CAMBRIDGE LIBRARY COLLECTION

Books of enduring scholarly value

Travel and Exploration

The history of travel writing dates back to the Bible, Caesar, the Vikings and the Crusaders, and its many themes include war, trade, science and recreation. Explorers from Columbus to Cook charted lands not previously visited by Western travellers, and were followed by merchants, missionaries, and colonists, who wrote accounts of their experiences. The development of steam power in the nineteenth century provided opportunities for increasing numbers of 'ordinary' people to travel further, more economically, and more safely, and resulted in great enthusiasm for travel writing among the reading public. Works included in this series range from first-hand descriptions of previously unrecorded places, to literary accounts of the strange habits of foreigners, to examples of the burgeoning numbers of guidebooks produced to satisfy the needs of a new kind of traveller - the tourist.

The Journal of Mr Samuel Holmes

This journal, kept by a soldier in the Light Dragoons of the voyage to 'China and Tartary' in the years 1792–3, was published in 1798. Holmes kept his diary during the attempt by Lord Macartney to establish an Embassy in China. Macartney returned to Britain unsuccessful, heightening western curiosity about this secluded and mysterious nation, and so this account by a soldier assigned to Lord Macartney's guard remains an important historical source on Europeans in China during this period. While, as the editor's preface admits, the text is not of great literary significance ('written by a worthy, sensible, but unlearned man'), its authenticity and soldier's-eye perspective make it a valuable document for historians today. The journal starts with H.M.S. *Lion* setting sail from Portsmouth, and ends with its return to British shores; the author notes diverse cultural features of the countries visited, and gives geographical references.

T0370862

Cambridge University Press has long been a pioneer in the reissuing of out-of-print titles from its own backlist, producing digital reprints of books that are still sought after by scholars and students but could not be reprinted economically using traditional technology. The Cambridge Library Collection extends this activity to a wider range of books which are still of importance to researchers and professionals, either for the source material they contain, or as landmarks in the history of their academic discipline.

Drawing from the world-renowned collections in the Cambridge University Library, and guided by the advice of experts in each subject area, Cambridge University Press is using state-of-the-art scanning machines in its own Printing House to capture the content of each book selected for inclusion. The files are processed to give a consistently clear, crisp image, and the books finished to the high quality standard for which the Press is recognised around the world. The latest print-on-demand technology ensures that the books will remain available indefinitely, and that orders for single or multiple copies can quickly be supplied.

The Cambridge Library Collection will bring back to life books of enduring scholarly value (including out-of-copyright works originally issued by other publishers) across a wide range of disciplines in the humanities and social sciences and in science and technology.

The Journal of Mr Samuel Holmes

*One of the Guard on
Lord Macartney's Embassy
to China and Tartary*

SAMUEL HOLMES

CAMBRIDGE
UNIVERSITY PRESS

CAMBRIDGE UNIVERSITY PRESS

Cambridge, New York, Melbourne, Madrid, Cape Town, Singapore,
São Paolo, Delhi, Dubai, Tokyo

Published in the United States of America by Cambridge University Press, New York

www.cambridge.org
Information on this title: www.cambridge.org/9781108013789

© in this compilation Cambridge University Press 2010

This edition first published 1798
This digitally printed version 2010

ISBN 978-1-108-01378-9 Paperback

THE

JOURNAL

OF

MR. SAMUEL HOLMES,

SERJEANT-MAJOR OF THE XIth LIGHT DRAGOONS,

DURING HIS ATTENDANCE, AS ONE OF
THE GUARD ON

LORD MACARTNEY'S

EMBASSY

TO

CHINA AND TARTARY.

1792—3.

PRINTED WITHOUT ADDITION, ABRIDGMENT,
OR AMENDMENT, FROM THE ORIGINAL
DIARY, KEPT DURING THAT
EXPEDITION.

LONDON:

PRINTED BY W. BULMER AND CO.

1798.

PREFACE

BY THE EDITOR.

———————————

MR. SAMUEL HOLMES, lately, from
merit, promoted to the rank of Serjeant-
Major of the 1 1 th Regiment of Dragoons,
was one of the Guard who attended LORD
MACARTNEY on his Embassy to China and
to Tartary, and kept a regular Diary of
what passed on the occasion, within the
sphere of his own knowledge and inquiries.
On careful perusal of this Diary or Journal,
it appears to bear every mark of authenticity, and to carry internal evidence of
its being written, as it professes to be, on

immediate and local impression from the objects and circumstances within the view of a person in the writer's situation. On such grounds, the Journal of a Voyage to China, written by a worthy, sensible, but unlearned man, is recommended to notice: on such ground it humbly rests;—and if therein *little* is added to the stock of intelligence already received of what was remarked, or what occurred, during the expedition alluded to, yet *that little* may not appear wholly uninteresting; and specially as it is presumed, from the character of the writer, to have the value of Truth, and that the curious reader may with confidence place it to his account of knowledge respecting that great and secluded nation, to which the inquiries of the politician and philosopher have been so long and much directed.

It was for the above reasons, and *for patronage of humble merit*, that it was proposed to print from this Diary or Journal a certain number of copies, for the libraries of the curious : and as no further publication or sale was intended, the subscription (though for a small octavo) was fixed at *One Guinea,*—in order to defray the expence of printing in a handsome manner, and to provide a residue acceptable to the worthy Author, in his present situation of life.

The book was directed to be entered at Stationers' Hall, in order to prevent sur-

reptitious editions, and to confine the possession of the work to the original Subscri-
bers; * and the original MS. on Indian
paper, will be deposited in the library of
the Royal Society.

For the further satisfaction and information of those who have so liberally pa-
tronized this little work, the Editor subjoins
a Letter from Serjeant-Major HOLMES,
in answer to questions relative to time,
place, and manner, in which the particulars
of this Journal were collected, and by him
committed to writing.

* The subscriptions received at Messrs. Knight
and Triphook's, stationers to the King, St. James's
Street.

*Copy of Serjeant-Major Holmes's Letter to Sir
W. Young, as to the manner in which his Journal was written.*

Reading, Berks, 7th Dec. 1797.

May it please your Honour,

In answer to your favour, this morning
received, I beg leave to acquaint you, that on
our leaving England I took a small book for the
purpose of making memorandums, not thinking to enlarge so much; but which I had completely filled by the time we landed in China.
I then bought the Chinese paper, and copied
from the above book; after which I inserted all
observations daily, and never wrote a line in
the book about China after leaving Macao; and
the only assistance I received was from one of
my comrades, who gave me the liberty of per-
using his journal, and he had the same liberty

[viii]

with mine, and the assistance from the log-book
for observations of latitude and longitude; and
had finished the book when I landed in England, except part of the last leaf.

I am, SIR, with great respect,

Your most obedient,

humble servant,

S. HOLMES,
Serjeant-Major 11th Dragoons.

Sir W. Young, Bart. M.P.

VOYAGE

TO

CHINA AND TARTARY.

O<small>N</small> Friday the 14th of September, 1792, the troops destined to accompany Lord Macartney, on his Embassy to the Court of Pekin, received orders to embark at Spithead, in the following order: twenty of the royal artillery, on board the Lion man of war of sixty-four guns, commanded by Sir Erasmus Gower; twenty infantry, and ten light dragoons, on board the Hindostan, a fine new Indiaman of 1200 tons burthen, under the command of Captain William Mackintosh.

On Tuesday the 25th, his Lordship and suite came on board, and on the follow-

B

ing day the ships weighed anchor, in company with several merchantmen bound to
the westward. On Thursday the 27th,
we saw the Isle of Wight, bearing east-
north-east, distant five leagues, it blowing
very hard from the south-west, the Jackall
brigantine, which was to accompany us,
being at this time far astern; on the following day we lost sight of her entirely,
and were apprehensive that some disaster
had happened to her, which had obliged
her to put back again to Portsmouth.

About noon we came to an anchor in
Torbay, where we continued till the 1st
of October, when a smart breeze springing up from the eastward, we weighed
anchor once more, and in a few hours lost
sight of our native country. Several ships
in sight, some homeward, some outward
bound. Early in the morning of the 3d,
we saw Ushant, on the coast of France,
bearing south-south-west, distant four

leagues. This, and for some following days we had light airs of wind and a heavy swell, setting across the Bay of Biscay. On the 4th, the Lion made a signal for us to carry more sail. On the 5th, we passed a Danish Indiaman standing to the eastward; and the following day we spoke a ship from Bristol bound to the coast of Africa.

On the 7th, we saw a large ship and cutter standing to the eastward; we had thick dirty weather, and squally On the 8th, the Lion sprung her fore-top-mast in crowding too much sail; we continued on our course, and left her astern repairing her damage. About five o'clock the same afternoon, we saw land ahead of us, and at daybreak on the 9th, we found ourselves near the rocks named the Desertas, which lay off the south-east of the island of Madeira, and found the south-east extremity of them to be in latitude

32° 33′ north, longitude 16° 17′ west of Greenwich.

About noon we came to an anchor in Funchal roads, and in the evening saw the Lion bearing up towards the island, but the wind being light she could not fetch it till next morning, when she came to an anchor alongside of us, and saluted the Governor with fifteen guns, which was returned from the fort by an equal number. The Governor had notice of our intention to touch here, and orders from Lisbon had been sent to him to treat the Embassador and his suite with every mark of attention and respect, which orders he punctually executed; lodgings and every other accommodation were provided on shore, to which they immediately repaired : his Lordship was saluted from the Lion and the forts on landing.

Liberty was given to the soldiers who

composed his Excellency's guard, to go on shore for several days, and they were treated with singular marks of attention by the inhabitants, who seemed eager to show them every thing worth notice; indeed nothing was wanting that this luxuriant island afforded, to give universal satisfaction.

The soil of Madeira is extremely fertile; it abounds in fruits of various kinds, particularly grapes, which are in such abundance as to enable them annually to export very considerable quantities of wine to all parts of Europe; it abounds also in game of different species, many of which are found in the warmer latitudes of Europe, and others peculiar to itself. There are a vast number of lizards in the island, but they say no venomous creatures were ever seen upon it. There is only one town of any note, but a vast number of delightful country seats, where the Portuguese spend the chief part of their time. There is also a great many convents and religious houses in all parts of the island, and in the most beautiful situations, surrounded by orange groves and evergreens of different kinds: During our continuance here, although the wind had been some time favourable, we saw nothing of the Jackall; we therefore began to despair of ever seeing her again.

On the 16th of October, we weighed anchor, receiving and returning the salute as upon our arrival; and without any material occurrence, on Sunday the 21st, we saw with pleasure the Peak of Teneriffe (supposed to be the highest single mountain in the world). It being a fine clear morning, we saw its summit very distinctly above the clouds. About noon we made the island of Teneriffe, and in the evening anchored in the road of Santa Cruz, after an excellent passage of only

three weeks, from England, including the
time we spent at Madeira. There is very
little to please a traveller at this place; he
has heard wonders of its celebrated Peak,
but he may remain for months together
at the town of Santa Cruz, without having a glimpse of it, and when its head is
free from the clouds, he is sure to feel
disappointed; for, from the point of view
in which he beholds it, the neighbouring
mountains lessen its effect very considerably; and except the Peak, the eye re-
ceives but little pleasure from the face of
the country, which is barren and uninvit-
ing to the last degree. The town, however, from its cheerful white appearance,
contrasted with the dreary brownness of
the mountains behind it, forms a pleasing
object; it is neither irregular in its plan,
nor despicable in its style of building. The
churches and religious houses are numerous, sumptuous, and highly ornamented,
but the restless importunity and impu-

dence of the beggars, and the immodesty of the lower class of women, are extremely disgusting.

As there are a considerable number of Englishmen settled at this place, we were not at a loss for society or information; it was indeed only from persons of this description we could obtain either, for it is very difficult to overcome the reserve of a Spaniard, especially by an Englishman, whose own is nearly equal.

The inland country is described as fertile and romantic, and the environs of the small town of Laguza, situated at the foot of the Peak, is particularly pleasant. Some of our officers and gentlemen made an excursion to the Peak, and endeavoured to gain the summit, but found the air so extremely cold, the ascent so dangerous, and so many other difficulties, that they were obliged to desist. Some of them, more adventurous than the rest, got within half a mile of the top, by climbing over rocks and precipices upon their hands and feet; but they then returned to the ships much fatigued and disappointed, after a week's absence from them. The Peak appears in the form of a sugar loaf, and its perpendicular height is said to be more than three miles; but it is a vulgar error respecting its top being perpetually covered with snow, as it is a white stone, much resembling it at a distance. There are some curious subterraneous caverns at the foot of the Peak, which supply the inhabitants of the island with ice the whole year round. The markets here afford fresh meat, but it is neither plentiful or good; fish is very scarce, but poultry may be procured in great abundance, and as cheap as in any of our English seaports. Vegetables do not abound, except pumpkins and onions, the latter of which are of a very mild na-

ture. Of fruits, they have grapes, figs,
oranges, and mulberries in great plenty
in their season. Wine is sold from ten
pounds four shillings to fifteen pounds per
pipe; and for the latter price the best
sort, which they call "London particular," may be had. Goats are bought
for a trifle, and easily procured: but the
voyager will do well to supply himself
plentifully with dollars before he quits
England, if he would insure a welcome
reception from the selfish Spaniards here.

The latitude of Santa Cruz is 28° 27'
north, and 16° 17' west from Greenwich.
In sailing from Teneriffe to the southward
the various appearances of the Peak are
beautiful to a degree; the stupendous
height which was before lost to the spec-
tator, now strikes him with awe and ad-
miration, the whole island appearing one
vast mountain with a pyramidal top;—
sometimes, with a light airy breeze, it is

seen for several successive days, and we
were credibly informed, that in clear weather it might be discerned at the distance
of an hundred miles; but we lost sight of
it altogether the next morning after our
departure, having a fine stiff breeze, which
carried us at the rate of ten miles an
hour.

We left Santa Cruz on the 27th of October, and the breeze continued favourable till we reached the Cape Verde
islands, which we saw on the evening of
November 1st, and next day, about noon,
came to an anchor opposite the town of
Port Praya. The Cape Verdes are a
cluster of small islands on the coast of
Africa, from which the principal, St. Jago,
is distant about 500 miles; they are eight
or ten in number, and in general afford
excellent water and beef for shipping;
the cattle are rather diminutive compared
with ours in England; but a good fat ox

may be bought for less than five dollars:
and fruit, such as oranges, lemons, cocoa
nuts, plantains, and bananas, &c. are in
such plenty that some of our sailors bought
considerable quantities of them for an old
jacket scarce worth a groat. These islands
produce but little grain of any kind; there
are some fine vallies, but they are parched
up for want of rain; we were told that
they had not had any rain for nearly five
years. The inhabitants are chiefly slaves
brought from the coast of Africa, and Portuguese transported for their crimes; so
that the Europeans you meet with here
are the very sweepings of the prisons, and
surely nothing can be more miserable than
their manner of living here; being near
the equinoctial line, the weather is into-
lerably hot; and though provision is in
such plenty, the whole is the property of
a few individuals, who find it their interest
to reserve it for the shipping, which continually call here for it. The wretched

slaves subsist upon fruit and fish, the latter very scarce and bad; and their huts are as miserable as their diet, being only loose stones piled together, and covered with cocoa-nut leaves. Of animals peculiar to these islands none were seen by us, except monkies, which are of a very small and beautiful yellow species, and not so very mischievous as those creatures generally are: there are also several species of wild fowl. The officers and gentlemen from our ships made some shooting excursions up the country, in which they were generally very successful; they brought on board several fine turkies and Guinea fowls, and one of them killed a fine large eagle, bald on the head and grey with age. Both Negroes and Portuguese are Roman Catholics, and very superstitious.

At St. Jago there is a chapel decently furnished, the officiating fathers are Negroes. There is a guardhouse and a few

Negro soldiers, miserably armed and worse cloathed; a few guns are mounted, but the walls are so indifferent, that a six-pound shot would demolish the whole. St. Jago is in latitude 15° north, and 35° 40′ west longitude.

On the 7th of November we weighed anchor, with a breeze from the south-east; we crossed the Equator on the 18th, with the usual and whimsical ceremonies of shaving and ducking those who never had crossed it before. In general you meet with calms and dreadful thunder and lightning near the line; but we passed it with a fine breeze, which invariably continued till we made the coast of America; and, what added to our satisfaction, all on board both ships were strong and healthy; no symptoms of the scurvy had yet appeared, owing to the great care and attention of good officers and experienced surgeons.

From the Equator our passage was in-
conceivably pleasant; the weather was
mild and serene, much like our finest
weather in England. The Lion was frequently obliged to shorten sail for us, and
but for that circumstance, would probably
have made her voyage to the Brazils much
shorter than she did; however we had no
reason to complain, as our voyage was
performed from St. Jago in twenty-four
days, which usually takes six weeks. On
the 30th of November we came to an
anchor in the harbour of Rio de Janeiro,
opposite the city of St. Sebastian, the
capital of the Brazils in South America.
The Lion saluted the Governor with fifteen guns, which was immediately returned; but it was a considerable time before
any of us could obtain leave to land. This
is the most valuable settlement belonging
to the Portuguese; it produces sugar, tobacco, cotton, hides, and valuable drugs
for medicine and manufactures; it also

affords gold, silver, and even diamonds; the gold alone, they say, annually exported to Europe, exceeds in value four millions sterling. The Viceroy has a palace here, which is large but not elegant, the city is strongly fortified, and there are many fortifications in different parts of the harbour; there are also several ships of war stationed here, and a respectable military force : the city is large and regular, but the buildings are rather mean, except the churches and religious houses, which are most superbly ornamented. There are numerous convents for the various religious sects of different persuasions, who appear to have much sanctity about them; though many of them do not scruple to commit the most desperate crimes. It is very dangerous and unsafe for a stranger to be amongst them, unless he is well acquainted with their manners and customs, and adheres strictly to them. The inhabitants are a people sunk in effeminate luxury, of a temper hypocritical and dissembling; insincere in conversation, and dishonest in dealing; superstitious, ignorant, rich, lazy, proud, and cruel, and, like the inhabitants of most southern climates, prefer show and state to the pleasures of society or a good table. When they visit each other, or appear abroad, they are too lazy and proud to walk even the most trifling distance, but are borne upon the shoulders of Negroes, in a kind of chair, richly ornamented; they have no other kind of carriage, and but very few horses. When a vessel arrives here, the master or commanding officer is obliged to give a very particular account of himself, from whence he came, and whither bound, &c. nor is any person suffered to land, till permission is obtained from the Viceroy, which is not done without difficulty and delay. The stranger is then taken like a prisoner to the guardhouse, and obliged to answer

C

any impertinent question the officer there may think proper to ask. If any thing, though of the most trivial nature, is brought on shore, it must be narrowly examined; nor is he suffered to walk about, without being accompanied by an officer, or soldier, who never quits him for a moment till he returns on board. The ladies here are handsome, and of an amorous constitution; they are not averse to strangers, but it is difficult and dangerous to get amongst them, as they are so strictly watched by the jealousy of the other sex, who do not fail to punish any slight transgression with the utmost severity; notwithstanding which, a stranger may, with a little trouble, satisfy all his wants at Rio de Janeiro, provided money is not one of them.

This place produces, in great abundance, variety of fruits. The climate is hot, boisterous, and unhealthy, subject to thunder,

lightning, rains, and variable winds, and
but for the sea breezes which blow in the
afternoon, would be intolerable. During
the time we lay here, which was in December, it was uncommonly hot; and we could
not help remarking that, at a time when
probably our friends in Europe were con-
triving to keep out the cold, we were
panting for breath, owing to the great
heat we endured. It was indeed here
the beginning of their summer; the
oranges and other fruits being nearly
ripe. We saw but few animals during
our stay here, but they were described
as being the same as found in Mexico
and Peru. We purchased some delicate
and beautiful little animals, somewhat
larger than a rat, of a red glossy colour, their feet and tail like those of a
monkey, but the head resembling a lion,
with long shaggy hair over its face; it
devoured its food like a monkey; but
was more sedate, and lived chiefly upon

C 2

fruit and milk, and could not bear the least cold.

The Hero, an English ship from the South Seas, arrived here a few days after us; she sailed for London a short time before we left the harbour; we sent numerous packets to our friends in Europe, and one sailor returned home in her who was ill, and very desirous to leave us, as he thought he should not be able to weather the fatigues of so long a voyage. We were sorry to remark, that at this place some little murmuring and discontent broke out amongst the soldiers on board the Hindostan, respecting some extra duty which had been imposed upon them by the officers in the ship; they had hitherto behaved remarkably well, and had been very useful in the ship. Colonel Benson, who commanded the party, reprobated their conduct in the most pointed terms; he represented the dangerous tendency of such behaviour, how injurious it would prove to themselves, and disgraceful to the whole party, who had so willingly volunteered themselves to guard the Embassy; and if any amongst them were dissatisfied, he offered them leave to return home in the Hero; but they all disdained the idea of returning in disgrace, and cheerfully submitted to conform to any orders he should give to forward the service. They had permission to go on shore at every place where the ship touched, and every indulgence granted them, that reasonable men could desire, and had certainly less reason to complain, than any party of soldiers that ever went on board before them.

Rio de Janeiro is in latitude 23° 30′ south, and 42° 13′ west longitude, from Greenwich.

On the 16th of December, his Lordship

and suite all came on board, and the following day we got out to sea once more, with a stiff breeze from the southward, and bore away east-south-east. On the 19th, the wind veered round to the eastward, and blew fresh; the weather from extremely hot, became chilling cold. On the 21st, the Lion sprung her fore-top-mast, and carried away her main-top-gallant mast. On the 22d, we spoke a Spanish brig from the Havannah, out three months, laden with rum, coffee, sugar, &c. bound for Rio Plata, in South America; and on the 23d spoke a Spanish sloop of war from Cadiz, bound for Lima. Towards evening we saw a brig under British colours, standing to the south-west; but it blowing fresh, and being hazy, could not speak her. The next day we had a smart gale from the eastward; it then cleared up, but we had lost sight of the Lion. We kept on the same course under all the sail we could carry, in expectation of falling in with her at the island of Tristan d'Acunha, which we expected to reach in the course of a week. The 25th we celebrated with all the festivity in our power, and were pretty joyous throughout the ship. About five in the afternoon, a sail was discovered from the mast-head, on our lee quarter, standing after us. We bore away, and hoisted a signal, which was immediately answered, and we presently discovered it to be the Lion ; we were now in the latitude of 35° south, and found the weather severely cold. Several of the soldiers on board were much afflicted with an inward complaint, which was occasioned by the sudden transition from heat to cold; but by proper attention it was removed, without producing any ill effect. On the 30th, in the evening, we discovered land, bearing east-south-east, distant near ten leagues. At daylight next morning both ships stood in towards it. At noon, the island of Tristan d'Acunha, distant two leagues; Inaccessible island, south-south-east, five leagues; and Nightingale island, south by west, six leagues. These three small islands, are about midway from Rio de Janeiro to the Cape of Good of Hope, in the latitude of 37° south, 14° 15′ west longitude. Tristan d'Acunha is the largest, and about eight miles in circumference; it is for the most part a barren rock, which appears at a distance in the form of a sugar loaf, very much resembling the Peak of Teneriffe, and in our opinion not much less in height. There is neither anchorage, shelter, or any inducement for ships to touch at these desert islands. In the afternoon, the Lion made a signal that she meant to come to an anchor, and sent out her boats to find out a proper situation. Towards evening it began to blow fresh, and had the appearance of being a tempestuous night, we therefore thought it prudent to stand off till morning. As we conjectured, so it happened. On the morning of the 1st of January, 1793, we saw the Lion at a great distance to leeward of the island, and bore away towards her; she had drifted in the night, and thinking it unsafe to make a second attempt, both ships bore away before a fine breeze, which carried us at the rate of ten miles an hour. In the neighbourhood of these islands we saw a great number of very large whales, and some few turtles. After this, nothing material happened till off the Cape of Good Hope, on the 7th, we were overtaken by a gale of wind, which blew with uncommon violence for six hours, and then suddenly died away; we found the wind in these latitudes very variable, blowing from every point of the compass in twenty-four hours, and for the most part thick, dirty weather. In the latitude of 39° south, and from 19° to 90° east longitude, we had repeated heavy gales, and frequently lost sight of the Lion for several days together, but were always fortunate enough to meet again. The latter part of this month we had light airs of wind and calms for several days.

Early in the morning of the 1st of February, a breeze springing up, we saw the island of St. Paul right ahead, distant six or seven leagues. In the afternoon we came to, in forty-five fathoms, on the north-east side of the island; on our nearer approach to it, we saw smoke issuing from several places on the higher land, which we at first supposed to be signals from some unhappy beings who had been shipwrecked here, but found, on landing, it was occasioned by volcanoes; in the day time we saw nothing but smoke, but at night, the flames burst out a prodigious height, in upwards of twenty different places; and the gentlemen who took a survey of the island described it as full of volcanic eruptions. The Hero was the first English ship that ever an-

chored at the island of Amsterdam, which
is in latitude 38° 43' south, and 78° 13'
east longitude. On our first landing, we
found the shore covered with such a mul-
titude of seals, that we were obliged to
disperse them, before we got out of the
boats. This island also abounds with
sea lions, of most enormous size and tremendous appearance, some of them mea-
suring twenty feet in length, and nearly
as much in circumference. These animals are of a dirty-white, or stone colour;
they are very inoffensive, and so unwieldy
and lazy as not to move at the approach
of any one, unless attacked, when they
retreat backwards towards the sea, with
their mouths open, and shaking their
heads, but without making any noise.
They are difficult to kill; for notwithstanding one of them received several
musket balls in his head, throat, and
body, so that the blood ran from him in
torrents, he found means to escape into

the sea. They greatly resemble the seal
in shape, and like them are furnished
with four feet or fins, the two hindermost
of which they sometimes erect, so as to
resemble a tail. On this truly miserable
isle, which is little known in Europe,
there were five persons, Americans and
Frenchmen, who had been left there eight
months before by a French vessel, to procure seal skins; and though they daily
destroyed one hundred and fifty seals, yet
there seemed to be no diminution of their
number. They could with ease have killed treble that number, had they been
able to preserve their skins. These men
were suffering very much for want of
some necessaries, the place affording nothing but fish; and they were to remain
twelve months longer, before the ship
was to fetch them away. For twenty
dollars, or their value in provisions, rum
or tobacco, they offered a thousand prime
skins. For prudential reasons, this advan-

tageous offer was rejected; but Captain Gower supplied them with several necessary articles gratis. The island is about seven miles in circumference, mostly high rugged land, without either tree or shrub, vegetable or animal productions. On the eastern side of it, there is a bason so completely formed, and sheltered from the wind by the surrounding hills, that it is as smooth as a pond, though thirty fathoms deep in the centre. It contained a variety of fish of the most delicious flavour, many of which we caught, and boiled (in a hot spring) so close to the edge of the bason, that you might put one foot in cold water and the other in scalding hot at the same time. The fish dressed in this manner were eaten by several of our people. Whatever credit this assertion may meet in Europe I know not, but it is an actual fact.

There were many other natural curiosi-

ties which we had not leisure to examine, as
we sailed on the evening of the 2d of February, with a smart westerly breeze. On
the 18th, we were in latitude 26° 30′ south,
and 103° east longitude, the westernmost
point of New Holland being, by our calculation, not more than two hundred miles
distant.

On account of the trade winds, which
blow invariably from the eastward, between the latitude of 30° north, and 30°
south, we stood much to the south-east;
but this day we spoke the Lion, and agreed
to bear away due north, concluding that
we had passed a ledge of breakers, called
the Trial Rocks, which lay off the south-
west end of New Holland; they are very
dangerous, being so far from any land,
and extending some miles in length, neither are they very accurately laid down.
They were first discovered by a Swedish
Indiaman, in the year 1760.

From this time the wind was moderate
but steady, and the weather, as we advanced towards the Line, became very sultry.
The Lion kept steering wide of us for several days, in expectation of falling in with
some of the homeward bound Indiamen.
On the 22d and 23d, she made different
signals to us; but being so far distant from
her, we could not distinguish their mean-
ing, and therefore kept standing on our
course. The 24th, we saw a great number of tropic birds and boobies, a sufficient demonstration of our being near
land. These boobies, or as some call
them, noddies, are so stupid and drowsy,
that when they alight on the shipping
(which they frequently do) the seamen
may go directly and take them, as they
fall asleep in a moment; one that we
caught had a flying fish in his mouth.

On the 25th, near dusk, we saw Java head, distant ten leagues. On the

26th, we entered the Straits of Sunda. About noon we saw a ship under British colours coming out, which, to our great satisfaction, proved to be the Earl of Wycombe, Captain Wood, an homeward bound Indiaman. By her we sent intelligence to our friends in Europe, of our having thus far weathered the voyage in safety. She informed us that we had been long expected; that she had brought dispatches from China to Lord Macartney, and staid fifteen days at Batavia, where she was ordered to wait our arrival; but the unhealthiness of the place and other circumstances, determined Captain Wood to leave the dispatches with the Dutch Governor, and to make the best of his way to Europe. She also had left letters for us at Angeree Point, and at North Island; and we had the satisfaction to learn that the dispatches to his Lordship were of a pleasing nature, with regard to our future reception from the Emperor,

which we were given to understand would
be as flattering, as the Embassy was singular and uncommon. After the usual
compliments, we left the Earl of Wycombe
to pursue her voyage, and in the evening
we came to an anchor off Angeree Point.
Between that place and Cocotore island,
on the coast of Sumatra, Lord Cathcart,
the only Embassador that England ever
before attempted to send to China, died
a few days before the ship entered the
Straits of Sunda. He was interred at Angeree Point, where a temporary monument was erected to his memory, and
some years afterwards the East India
Company sent out a very elegant marble
one to be put up, describing his age, title,
and service he was going upon, which
miscarried, no secondary person being
appointed.

On the 27th, we weighed anchor early
in the morning, and had light breezes of

D

variable wind and calms. At noon, we
spoke a large Dutch Indiaman, homeward bound; and in the evening, an
American ship and brig, bound for Ostend; the ship laden with sugar from
Canton, the brig was in ballast; the captain, who was owner of both, intended to
dispose of her before his arrival in Europe.
He had sailed in her from Boston, in
the United States, and had made several
beneficial trips between China and the
south-west coast of America, in the fur
trade, by which he had gained an ample
fortune. He had purchased the ship in
some part of Asia, and laden her with
sugar to return to Europe.

Captain Mackintosh had some intention to purchase the brig, in lieu of the
Jackall, which we had given up all hopes
of seeing again; but as they could not
agree upon terms, we parted. At night
we anchored off Cocotore island, and

the following day we came to in fifteen fathoms, between North Island and
Sumatra, which is the usual place where
our China ships take in wood and water.

A Javanese proa came off to us with
turtle, fruit, fowls, birds, and monkies: the
turtle afforded us a very agreeable repast,
after being so long confined to salt provisions. The next day the Lion hove in
sight, and in the afternoon anchored
alongside us: she had not seen the Earl
of Wycombe Indiaman, nor any of the
other ships we had spoke with, and had
very nearly been ashore to leeward of
Java head.

The island of Sumatra has Malacca on
the north, Borneo on the east, and Java
on the south-east, from which it is divided
by the Straits of Sunda; it is reckoned
about one thousand miles in length, and
one hundred in breadth, and is divided

into two equal parts by the Equator, extending five degrees north-west and five
degrees south-east of it.

The English East India Company have
two settlements upon it near the Straits
of Malacca;-Bencoolen and Fort Marlbo-
rough.   The interior parts of the island
are governed by Pagan princes, who are
always at enmity with Europeans, and
generally with each other; they were represented to us as cannibals. They live
in small villages fortified with camphor
planks, and sharp pointed stakes driven
into the ground, covered with long grass
or weeds: those who inhabit the shore
are called Malays; they are of a dark
olive colour, of a middle size, but generally short; their hair and eyebrows black,
their eyes and noses little, their mouths
large, and few of them have any beard;
they appear civil, grave, simple, and will-
ing to oblige. Some of them came off

to us, but seemed very shy, and undetermined whether to look upon us as enemies or friends; they offered us cocoa-
nuts, plantains, chickens, buffaloes, turtles, and matting; for which they wanted
old shirts, handkerchiefs, knives, &c.
When they salute you, they say *taba tuani*,
or good day to you. Their huts consist
of four poles driven into the ground,
and covered with cocoa leaves at the top,
but open at the sides; and in the middle of it a kind of bench is erected, covered
with leaves and matting, upon which they
sleep: they want no chairs, as they sit upon
their heels, like monkies. They go almost
naked, having nothing but a brown cotton
cloth spotted with blue tied round their
bodies with a handkerchief, in which they
wear a kind of dagger, like a long kitchen
knife, the point of which they generally
poison : they are continually chewing the
betle-nut, or something of that sort,
which makes their teeth black, and their

lips and mouth as red as fire: round their
long black hair they wear a thin striped
cloth, but tied in such a manner that the
crown of their head remains uncovered.
They were represented to us as very
treacherous and deceitful, and that it was
dangerous to go amongst them unarmed;
I believe they had, a few months before,
cut off a boat's crew belonging to an Indiaman. We seldom at first omitted every
necessary precaution; but, by degrees,
our suspicion began to wear away, as they
appeared so harmless, and desirous to
please. Most of the soldiers, who had
permission to go on shore, straggled
carelessly amongst them, without any
weapon of defence : except some of them
a piece of bamboo, which they picked up
more as a curiosity than by way of defence. They found one of their villages
at a little distance through the woods,
the inhabitants of which gathered round
them in amazement, wondering I sup-

pose, whether they were earthly or celestial beings that had so suddenly invaded their retreat; they however followed them with apparent wonder to the shore, without offering the least molestation, though they had frequently an opportunity of cutting some off, as our people were so eager to see and obtain any little curiosity that offered, that they very often separated into small parties. We bought a number of beautiful birds from these people; but they were tender, and most of them died soon after being carried on board. Monkies they have vast numbers, but the ugliest animals I ever beheld; they are about the size of a cat, of a light greyish colour, with a tuft on the top of their heads, below the belly is a little whitish, the snout is narrow, their nails are very long, and they have a beard; they embrace, and greet each other with a thousand grimaces, and will play with dogs if they have no nearer friend about them;

they are very uneasy when first separated
from their own species; if any body looks
cross at them they are very angry, and
begin a smacking noise with their teeth.
They resemble all other monkies I have
seen, in dirtiness, drollery and lascivious-
ness; if you let them go about freely,
they play a thousand tricks, jump over
every thing, steal away the people's meat,
hunt after chickens, break the necks of
birds, and carry mischief wherever they go.

The country hereabout was very high,
except near the shore, and the wood
so very thick, that it was with difficulty we could pass through; and were
obliged to keep near each other for fear of
not meeting again; the cries of birds,
lizards, and other noises, would not permit us to hear each other though we
called ever so loud; and another danger
we dreaded more, was being attacked by
beasts of prey, as it is said these woods

are infested with them, particularly tigers. The low swampy lands near the shore were full of reptiles of various sorts, and thousands of alligators, many of which we saw from ten to twelve feet long.

The largest sharks in the world are found in these straits; of three different sorts and colours; the black one is the largest and most voracious.

On the 4th of March, having completed our stock of water, and being anxious to get to Batavia, we weighed anchor at noon, after leaving the names of our ships, &c. at the watering-place, and on North Island, to inform the homeward bound Indiamen, which were expected from Canton, that if they should touch here in our absence, to wait our return, which would not exceed fifteen days; as by them we were to send dispatches to Europe.

An American ship, called the Columbus, a brig, and a schooner, anchored in
the straits just as we got out; they were
from Canton, and brought us intelligence
that the Sullivan was appointed to sail for
London the 10th instant.

Just before dark we got amongst a
cluster of low woody islands, called the
Ten Thousand Isles; and they are properly so called, being almost innumerable,
and extending on all sides as far as the
eye could reach. We had a fresh breeze
in our favour, but were obliged to anchor
till daylight to get safely through them:
we got up our anchor early next morning.
At noon we were abreast of Enroost, at
the entrance of Batavia harbour, and saw
a Chinese junk standing in for that place.
It is impossible to express the pleasure that
appeared to agitate the two Chinese on
board our ship, when they first discovered

one of their own country vessels; nor can
it be wondered at, when it is considered
they had been absent about fifteen years.
The junk kept pretty close to us as we
went in, and considering her awkward
shape, sails, &c. she blundered forward
remarkably fast. We got into Batavia
at five in the afternoon, and were saluted
by several British vessels which lay in
the harbour. There were near fifty sail
of Dutch vessels, some of them very
large; several French ships, and five or
six of the English East India Company's
trading vessels; beside ten or twelve
Chinese junks, and an innumerable
quantity of small craft. The morning
after our arrival, the Lion saluted the
Governor with thirteen guns, which
was immediately returned from the fort;
and his Excellency being informed that
Lord Macartney was somewhat indis-
posed, and could not conveniently go
on shore, was pleased to dispense with

ceremonials, and went himself on board
the Lion to welcome his Lordship to Batavia : he was. saluted by the shipping as
he passed and repassed.   The following
morning, being the birthday of the Prince
of Orange, a royal salute was fired from
the town and shipping.   About noon his
Lordship and suite went on shore, and
were received with every possible mark of
distinction.   The city of Batavia is in
latitude 6° 10″ south, and 105° east longitude; on the north-west side of the island
of Java, at the entrance of the river Ja-
cata, and furnished with one of the finest
harbours in the world.   The city itself is
nearly two leagues in circumference, and
surrounded with regular fortifications; the
suburbs are ten times more extensive, and
inhabited by natives from every corner of
the world, particularly Chinese, who alone
are said to amount to one hundred thousand.   The active tradesmen and mechanics are of that nation, being better

able to bear the heat of the climate than Europeans; they are very active and industrious, and contribute much to the riches of the place. The Dutch Viceroy of the Indies has his residence here, and when he appears abroad, is attended by his guards and officers, and a retinue far surpassing in splendour any European potentate.

The city is as beautiful as it is strong, and its fine canals, bridges, and avenues, render it a most agreeable residence; the streets are broad and well paved, the houses are large and elegantly furnished, they are built chiefly of brick. The citadel, where the Viceroy has a noble palace, commands the town and suburbs; there are besides a great number of public and private buildings, which exceeded in grandeur any I ever saw; in short, this is by numbers accounted the handsomest city in Asia, though it is allowed to be the most unhealthy. A Dutch garrison of three thousand men, constantly resides at Batavia; fifteen thousand other troops are quartered on the island and neighbourhood of the city. There is a very great mortality amongst those who are obliged to do duty in the garrison; we were assured, from indisputable authority, that no less than seventy-eight thousand six hundred men had died here in the space of sixteen years, and of thirty men who were appointed to attend Lord Macartney on shore, seven died in the course of four days! There are various opinions respecting the causes of the great mortality here; but it is chiefly attributed to the new arrack, of which new comers, particularly soldiers and sailors, generally take an immoderate allowance. The ground on which the city is built is low and swampy; the heat is excessive, though greatly tempered by a fine sea breeze from ten to four o'clock, and there may be

other natural causes which we are unac-
quainted with; but I am persuaded a tem-
perate man, who has been a little used to
the climate, may live here as safely as in
any part of the world.

The soil produces rice and grain of
different sorts, pepper, cinnamon, camphor, &c. besides a variety of fruits of
the most delicious flavour, and in great
plenty: the pine apples here are the finest
in the world, and in amazing abundance;
you may purchase almost an hundred for
a dollar: sugar, coffee, tea, sweetmeats, &c.
are also very cheap. Fowls you may buy
twelve for a dollar. Indeed most things
are reasonable except wine and beer,
which you must pay extravagantly for.
Their beef or buffaloes are but indifferent;
they are small, and have a large hump
between their shoulders. Pork is pretty
good, though small. Goats are in great
plenty, but we saw no sheep. The na-

tives eat but little animal food, rice and
Indian corn being their chief diet. The
prettiest birds in the universe are found
on the island of Java, and the neighbouring isles, but so delicate and tender they
cannot bear any cold; they are not musical, but some of them can repeat very
distinctly any thing they hear.

The natives of this island, of Sumatra,
and the neighbourhood, are Malays, nor
is there any difference in their persons,
manners, or customs. The greatest part
of Java is subject to the Dutch, though
they have several princes of their own all
in a great measure slaves to the Dutch.
We expected a visit from the King of
Bantam, on our crossing the bay to Batavia, but were disappointed; he is the
most powerful chief on the island; and had
expressed a great desire to see the English
Embassador, in hopes, I suppose, of a rich
present. Early on the 17th of March

we weighed anchor, and got down to
Enroost about noon, where we were becalmed. This is an island about nine miles
from Batavia, where their ships are generally hove down and repaired; the Lion
got aground near this place, but presently
hove off again without damage. We anchored this evening in Batavia bay. Sir
Erasmus Gower and Capt. Mackintosh,
had been in treaty with the owner of a
French brig at Batavia, and it being now
agreed to purchase her, a signal was made
for her to come down to us; she came
down on the 19th, and anchored under the
Lion's stern; she was a very handsome
vessel, and promised to be of great utility
to us in navigating the Chinese seas;
she was called the Clarence; and the
master's mate was appointed to command
her; the crew, which consisted of fifteen
men, were taken from the Lion. The 20th
we were busied in getting her ready for
sea, and the next morning early we

E

weighed anchor, and passed through a
cluster of small beautiful islands, inhabited chiefly by Dutchmen and Malays.
In the afternoon we spoke a ship from
Ostend, called the Achilles, bound for
Batavia, out five months; she brought
little intelligence from Europe; but what
was very interesting to us, she assured us,
that the Jackall had sailed from St. Jago
in pursuit of us a few days before they
had arrived there, and that she would
probably be in the Straits in a day or
two. On Thursday night we came too,
once more in our old birth between North
Island and Sumatra, where we were to
wait the arrival of the ships from China,
and the shifting of the monsoons, (a
kind of trade wind that blows from
the southward from April to September, and the other six months from the
northward). On Friday morning we
discovered a sail standing into the bay,
which we presently discovered to be our

little brig the Jackall. Boats were immediately sent from each ship to tow her in,
there being but little wind. She informed
us, that she had through stress of weather,
been obliged to put back to Spithead;
where having lain a few days, she again
put to sea, in hopes of coming up with us at
Madeira, where she arrived about a week
after we had left it; from thence she proceeded to St. Jago, where being equally unsuccessful, she bore away towards the Cape
of Good Hope : but having met with very
unfavourable winds, had been driven to
the southward, and was obliged to make
towards the Straits, where she happily arrived to our very great joy. They had
been much distressed for liquor and provisions, and she proved but an indifferent
sailer. On the 24th, some of our gentlemen went to Angeree Point, to see the
tomb of Lord Cathcart. The monument
had not been destroyed, but the inscrip-
tion was scarcely legible. On Monday

the 25th, the old Lord North, a country
ship, put in here, from China, bound for
Bombay, she had been out three months.
About this time a putrid fever began to
make its appearance in both our ships (the
Lion and Hindostan), which exceedingly
alarmed us; we had all hitherto been very
healthy. On the 27th the captain's cook
fell a sacrifice to it, after only two or three
days illness, and was buried the same afternoon on North Island.

On the following day, we had a melancholy proof of the savage disposition of
these islanders; a joiner and draughtsman
in his Excellency's suite, being on shore
washing some linen, happening to be
left alone by his comrade, who had wan-
dered a little into the woods, and had un-
fortunately taken both the fowling-pieces
with him, and not suspecting any foul play
from the natives, who had hitherto behaved so civilly, was cruelly butchered by

them; he had received several stabs in
different parts of his body, and was found
in the river by his comrade, who had not
been absent half an hour; but the savages
had decamped with all his linen, which
was supposed to be their principal inducement to commit this horrid murder. Several men well armed, were immediately
sent on shore, with orders to punish, with
death, any Malays they could find: they
had got into the back parts of the country,
and no opportunity offered of revenging
his death during our stay. We had, however, great reason to be thankful it was not
worse; the soldiers had escaped, I might
say, miraculously. I was on shore with a
small party of my comrades, on the 24th,
we were on the same business (washing
linen), quite unarmed, and surrounded by
the natives, but they offered us no molestation; on the contrary, they struck a
light for us to light our pipes, with a flint

and steel, and a bit of sponge, that caught
the sparks like tinder. They have a very
complete little box, made of cane, that
holds all the implements for smoking:
they use a kind of weed, or thin paper,
which they roll the tobacco in, and smoke
it as we would a pipe, and call it a segar.
The box is buckled round their waist, and
placed before them as we do our cartridge
boxes. They had every one a knife, which
they allowed us to take out of the sheath;
some of them were for cutting of wood,
others for their use in war. They were
very fond of chewing our tobacco: during the day to engage their affections, or
prevent hostility, we let them taste of our
rum; but they made signs that it burnt
their insides, and would not be persuaded
they were not poisoned, till we drank freely
ourselves. On Saturday the 30th, one of
the seamen died, and was buried the same
day on North Island.

On the 31st we weighed anchor, in
company with the Jackall, to go in search
of buffaloes on the island of Java. A
large French ship, which we had seen the
preceding day off the east end of Sumatra,
entered the Straits, and anchored alongside the Lion; she was from Manilla,
bound to Europe. About noon we anchored in a small pleasant bay near St.
Nicholas' Point, on the island of Java.
In the evening a servant of Mr. Hickey
the landscape painter died, and was buried
the following morning, on a small island
near St. Leonard's Point. At this time
the fever began to alarm us exceedingly,
a great number of petty officers and seamen being in a dangerous way; of the
latter upwards of thirty were incapable of
duty. The utmost precaution was taken
to prevent its spreading further. The
soldiers hitherto had been remarkably
healthy, though the part of the ship they
occupied was much the most confined,

and had not been properly cleaned from
filth and dirt since their embarkation at
Spithead.

On Monday, April 1, the Jackall was
dispatched to Angeree Point for buffaloes,
but returned in the evening without
making the Point. She succeeded the following day, and brought intelligence that
the Lion and Clarence were there, taking
in as many buffaloes as they could procure.
On Wednesday they both came down, and
sent us eight buffaloes for a present supply; we also got a supply of fowls from
Bantam. Captain Mackintosh waited upon
the King of that place, and informed him
of the murder which had been committed
by the Malays at Sumatra, and earnestly
entreated he would use his utmost endeavour to find out and punish the party who
were guilty. He promised to do all that
lay in his power for that end; and he hoped
before the ships departed they would have

the satisfaction to see the poor man's
death amply revenged.

On Thursday night the 24th at ten
o'clock, we weighed anchor, and at three
the next morning regained our old station
at North Island; we there found the ship
Achilles from Ostend, we had formerly
spoke with; she was wooding and watering for a voyage to Canton, and informed
us that on their first landing, they were surrounded by a large party of Malays, armed
with long spears, who asked what ship,
or what nation they belonged to; a few
Dutchmen who had entered at Batavia,
and understood the Malay tongue, answered they were Dutchmen; upon this
they were permitted to fill their water
casks. The villains were particularly anxious to find out if they had any knowledge
of, or connection with us, describing the
place where we lay, and fearing (as was
supposed) that they were sent with an

intention to seize some of them. Our
boats were sent next morning well armed
to the watering-place, but not a single
native could be seen : they had fled into
the interior part of the country, and had
turned the course of the water, to prevent
our getting a supply. The indignation
of all on board was raised to such a pitch,
that I believe they would have destroyed
every Malay on the island if they could
have got them in their power : we were
detained three days in filling twenty casks,
for which before, three or four hours
were sufficient. On the 8th, several of
our people assisted those from the Imperial ship to cut wood near the watering-
place, in hopes that the natives would
come down, but none appeared during
our stay.

On Monday morning we weighed anchor once more, and at noon came to
alongside of the Lion, near Java. A vast

number of proas were seen standing across
the Straits towards North Island, but they
kept a great distance from us. The long
boat was dispatched several times to
Bantam, and returned with a plentiful
supply of buffaloes. A canoe from the
shore ventured twice with some fish and
a little fruit, which was purchased, in the
hope it might induce others to come with
a more liberal supply; but whatever was
the cause, no other ever ventured near us.
From the place where we lay at anchor,
we had an imperfect view of a Malay
village, consisting of about thirty huts,
surrounded by large fields of paddy, apparently in a fine state of cultivation, as
far as the eye could reach. The prospect
was charming; besides the village above-
mentioned, we could discern a great number of huts, on the sides of the hills, each
situated in the centre of a fine green field;
they seemed very small, and were built in
the same manner as those at Sumatra.

On Thursday the Lion weighed anchor, and stood away to North Island, and the two brigs to Angeree Point. On Saturday the 14th, we saw two large ships under British colours, bearing up towards Angeree Point, which we supposed were the Sullivan and Royal Admiral, from China. In the evening died Wm. Harrington, a soldier belonging to Lord Macartney's guard. The next day we weighed anchor, and in the evening came too off Angeree Point, where we found the Lion, our two brigs, the two Indiamen, and an Imperial ship from China. On Monday the letters and dispatches for England were sent on board the Indiamen, who sailed in the evening. Several of our sick seamen were sent to England in them, and five Chinese pilots came to return home with us. The Indiamen they piloted meeting with a gale of wind off Macao, were obliged to bear away, and could get no opportunity to put them

ashore till they arrived here. They had
been a month from Canton. At Angeree
Point we took in a supply of water and
buffaloes, and procured plenty of fowls
and fruit, at very reasonable rates. The
natives here were not so shy as we had
found them at other places, as they have
several Dutchmen settled amongst them,
who make a point of going on board
every vessel that anchors in the Straits,
to get particulars of her name, destina-
tion, &c. for the sake of affording useful
information to others who may afterwards touch here. There is a battery, on
which a few guns are mounted, but they
are in very bad repair. The village is
pretty large and regular; the inhabitants,
who are chiefly Malays, may amount to
near 400. The country round about it, to
a considerable distance, is well cultivated,
and divided into regular inclosures, or
fields of rice, and Indian corn.

On Thursday the 19th the Lion hove
out a signal for us to weigh anchor, which
we obeyed with alacrity, being anxious to
get away from this place, and proceed on
our voyage; but having an unfavourable
wind, were obliged to drop anchor once
more off North Island, where we continued till the 21st. On Sunday the 28th
we arrived in the Straits of Banca, where
we had the misfortune to get aground,
but after two or three hours hove off again
without damage: these Straits are formed
by the islands of Sumatra and Banca, and
are considered as the entrance into the
Chinese sea.

Banca is a large island, and mostly
high land, covered with thick wood. The
Dutch have a large settlement upon it,
from which they send large quantities of
block tin to different parts of Asia; of its
other productions I have but a very im-

perfect knowledge, as the place where we lay at anchor was entirely uninhabited. Its animal productions are nearly the same as in the neighbouring islands of Java and Sumatra.

On our first landing at Banca, we discovered the tracks of wild hogs upon the beach, and heard several of them in the woods; but could not get within gun shot of them. We wooded and watered our ships here, at some small islands, called the Nanka Isles, and during our stay we discovered a great number of large piratical proas cruizing about the Straits; but they were careful to observe a proper distance from us, as we had too formidable an appearance for them. These vessels are large, but ill constructed, and have generally a nine or twelve pounder mounted in the bows, and some of them carry 18 or 20 swivels. They seldom venture to attack a square rigged vessel, unless

they think she has no guns to defend herself with, and even then they surround her
with not less than 30 or 40 of their vessels, the largest carrying from 60 to 100
men. They were impudent enough, while
we lay in the Straits of Sunda, to attack
a Dutch brig of 18 guns in Bantam Bay,
though several European ships were in
sight; but it being calm, they could not
get to her assistance, and want of wind
also prevented the brig from getting her
guns to bear upon them. They damaged
the rigging of the Dutch vessel very much,
and had not a breeze then sprung up, the
conflict would have been doubtful; but
this enabled the brig to beat them off.
When the weather is calm they make use
of oars, and can row a great number;
this gives them a considerable advantage
over small European craft, and enables
the proas to elude pursuit. All the rivers,
straits, and harbours, in the Chinese seas
are infested with them to such a degree,

that no vessel can venture there, unless well provided with the means of defence.

On the 3d of May we got up our anchor, having a fair wind for running through the Straits. About noon the Imperial ship Achilles, from Ostend, hove in sight, and at night came too alongside of us. The next morning we weighed, and stood over towards Monopon Hill, on the Banca side. The next day one of our seamen died. The fever, which had been so long and violent on board, had not proved fatal to many persons, and at this time rather abated; but the flux succeeded it, and threatened more dreadful consequences; it was generally attributed to the water we took in at the last place; it had a very pleasant taste, and the weather being so immoderately hot, we all drank freely out of the first supply, and the next day this disorder was general throughout each ship. When we were in the cold

F

latitudes off the coast of Africa, we were all
eager to get near the Equinoctial; and that
wish gratified, we were ten times as anxious to get away from it: but we had continued here an immoderate length of time
on one account or other, and it was no
wonder we were tired, considering the
many disagreeable circumstances we had
to encounter, such as sickness, deaths, un-
wholesome food, and many others not
proper to mention. Here the weather was
uncommonly hot, and seldom a day passed without rain, thunder, or lightning.
A disagreeable rash broke out all over us,
which we called the " prickly heat," from
the manner in which it pained us, being
compared to the pricking of pins all over
us; the bodies of some amongst us was
one entire sore from head to foot, and as
it afflicted us most when heated, we could
neither eat, drink, or sleep, with any comfort between decks, and it were dangerous to attempt to sleep on deck. To cheer

our present sufferings, we were encou-
raged with the assurances that these
things would wear away, and more pleasing scenes succeed them, as we advanced
to the northward, otherwise despair would
nearly have driven us all mad. On Monday the 6th we passed by the Seven
Islands, and anchored in the evening about
two leagues to the north-east of them.
This and the two following nights we had
heavy squalls of wind, with thunder, lightning, and rain. On the morning of the
8th Pulo Taya bore from west to north-
north-east from us. At 10 o'clock we
spoke the Jackall and Clarence, to make
sail ahead till they got close under land,
or into shoal water. At noon the Jackall
made a signal that she had only three fathoms, when the easternmost point of the
largest island bore north-east by east, distant two leagues; and the easternmost
point of high land of Linden island north-
west five leagues. Both brigs then stood

away to the westward, to endeavour to
find some harbour or commodious anchorage; but returned without being able to
accomplish it, the water being too shallow
to admit ships of any size to come near
the land. Towards evening we anchored
about three leagues from the largest island.
The two brigs stood away to the westward
once more, the boats were also sent out,
but with no better success than before:
the grand point was to find out some safe
and commodious harbour where shipping might be secured from danger during the shifting of the monsoons, that
they might not be forced to put back to
Batavia, as they very frequently are. The
violent gales that generally accompany
a change of wind are dreadful, beyond
imagination, in the Chinese seas, and are
too often attended with dangerous consequences to trifle with. These islands
lay very convenient, they are large, and
the land high, and to all appearance might

answer the desired end; but as far as we
had examined, which was the western side
only, the water was too shallow. Captain
Cook in one of his voyages had slightly
examined the largest of them, and judged
they might prove very advantageous, either
in peace or war: this I believe induced
the present adventurers to pay more extraordinary attention than otherwise they
would have done. The seamen and soldiers in general were very much dissatisfied at being detained so unnecessarily, as
they thought, in this unhealthy latitude.
They were dropping off very fast. On
board the Lion two died this day, and
numbers were expected not to survive
them long; they had 120 in the sur-
geon's list, all of them unfit for duty.
The centre of the island of Linden lay in
about 33 minutes south latitude, and 105
degrees east longitude.

The Clarence joined us early on the

morning of the 9th; the Jackall was
scarcely in sight to the westward. About
noon she bore down, and informed us that
she had not been able to find any harbour
where ships of any size could lay in safety:
we therefore weighed anchor in the evening, and stood out to sea. This day F.
Kelly, a seaman, departed this life, and
at sunset his body was committed to the
deep, in the usual manner. On the morning of the 10th, to our great joy, we
crossed the Equator to the northward,
but we found little alteration in the heat
of the weather. We kept standing north-
north-west, with a gentle breeze and fine
moderate clear weather. Before sunrise
on the 12th we discovered land ahead of
us, bearing north-north-east. At daylight we passed between Saddle Island
and the White Rock, the Great Anambas
north by east, distant five leagues; latitude by observation this day 4° 36′ north.
At four o'clock in the afternoon we passed

by Pulo Dorman, a large coral rock,
which at a distance had the appearance
of an ancient Gothic castle ; it was very
lofty, and the top was covered with something green. At five o'clock in the morning of the 16th we saw Pulo Condore, or
the island of Condore, *pulo*, in the Malay
tongue, signifying an island. At noon
we anchored in an open bay on the north-
east side of Condore, formed by that, and
several other islands within gun-shot of
it, called the Brothers ; the largest of
which does not exceed a league in circumference ; they are all mountainous and
rocky, except just on the edges of the
shore. The English had formerly a settlement on Pulo Condore; but putting too
much confidence in some Macassar soldiers, they were all inhumanly murdered ;
and no European power hath since thought
it worth attention. Its produce, I believe,
is very insignificant, and there are a few
Malays upon it, some say 1400 or 1500,

and others, that they do not exceed 100;
which latter I am rather inclined to credit, as I do not think so great a number
as the other could exist upon it. They
have some buffaloes, and we were told,
hogs and turkies; but we could procure
none of either, except buffaloes, and them
so lean and poor that they were not thought
worth carrying on board. Fish were also
scarce amongst them, as were fruit and
vegetables. The latitude of Pulo Condore is 8° 36' north, and 107° 22' east
longitude. The next morning when our
boats were sent on shore, they found all
the people had deserted their huts by the
side of the shore, and taken every thing
along with them, not so much as a hog
or a fowl remaining behind. What had
induced them to act in this unaccountable
manner, we could not guess, as we had
carried the most friendly appearance; but
as they are naturally mischievous and
treacherous themselves, probably they

dreaded that we might not be sincere in our professions. With much searching we found one or two old men, but we could get no information from them, and therefore the boats all put off from this inhospitable shore; but before they could reach their respective ships a most violent gale of wind came on. All got safe on board with some difficulty. The Lion made a signal for all the vessels to weigh anchor; the brigs answered that they were unable to comply with it. We endeavoured to heave up, but before we had got in many fathoms of cable, the messenger broke, and the capstan flew round with such violence, that all the efforts of the men were made to seek their own safety by deserting it entirely; but not before a corporal of his Lordship's guard had his thigh broke, a sailor his arm, and a great number of sailors and soldiers were severely bruised. Upwards of twenty were rendered unfit for duty. This

unlucky accident put a stop to all business for some hours ; mean while the gale
kept rapidly increasing. Captain Mackintosh being very averse to lying so much
exposed, declared his resolution was to get
out to sea before night at all hazards, and if
we could not purchase the anchor, to cut
away; however we were saved that trouble,
for in less than an hour the cable parted
about 30 fathoms from the anchor : this
determined all at once; and we were out
at sea in a moment ; but endeavoured to
keep the bay open all night, in case any
of the other vessels should venture, or be
driven out, and kept firing rockets frequently, to give them notice whereabouts
we were. The night proved dark and
squally, and in the morning we found
ourselves six leagues to leeward of the
bay, and had thick dirty weather. At
ten we saw the Lion, and a few moments
after the two brigs, coming out; we lay
too till they joined us, and then put away

right before the wind, which carried us
at the rate of nine or ten knots all the
day. Early the next morning we made
Cape James, on the coast of Cochin-
China, which is laid down in 10° 42′ north
latitude.

We had a very pleasant run all along
the coast, the wind being moderated, and
the weather as fine as we could wish
it to be, except being a little too sultry.
The land on the coast was in general
hilly, but appeared well cultivated, and
we judged pretty well inhabited. We saw
several junks and small fishing vessels.
On the 25th we saw the entrance into
Turon Bay, and a surprising number
of boats a fishing all round it. We sent
our jolly boats on board some of the nearest, with one of the Chinese pilots, who
we imagined would probably understand
their language sufficiently to be understood, and endeavour to persuade one of

them to pilot us in. They understood each
other but very imperfectly, and no arguments were sufficient to induce any of
them to come nearer to us; the boats
therefore came back with only a few
flying fish: another of the country boats
coming pretty close under our stern, in
which were two very young, and one
very old man, we first tried mild arguments, and shewed them dollars; but being as stiff as the others, the poor old
fellow was brought on board by force:
he appeared to be about ninety years of
age, though strong and vigorous. His
surprise when brought on board seemed
to take the power of speech from him for
some moments. When he had a little recovered himself, he burst out into such immoderate and violent fits of grief that astonished us all. He would lean over that
side of the vessel next the land, to which
he would point, and make motions that
he wanted to get there, while the tears

would burst from him in such agony, that none, even the most hardened sailor on board, could avoid being concerned for him, and some there were that thought it a piece of cruelty to detain the poor old fellow. The captain and officers endeavoured to dissipate his fears; but as signs and tokens were the only means they had to make their wishes known, nothing could subdue his sorrow. They gave him dollars, and offered him wearing apparel, seeing he was almost naked, but he would not touch them. The Chinese pilots were very officious ; they boiled him rice, and made different messes that they thought would please him, and at night tried to make him joyous : he eat but little, and slept none.

The 26th we saw none of the numerous fishing boats we had seen the preceding days, so that we apprehended the country would be alarmed, and we should

not be able to procure any thing we wanted. The current, during the night, had
driven us to the southward of the bay,
and the wind being contrary, we were
obliged to work up again. When the
ship's head lay towards the land, the old
man dried up his tears; but when we were
forced to tack and stand out, then would
they burst out afresh, and he cry like a
child. But upon the whole, he seemed a
little more easy this day Presently the
wind veered round, and we had a fine stiff
breeze setting right into the harbour;
we stood almost to the bottom of a fine
deep bay, the largest and most completely
sheltered from wind I almost ever saw,
where the whole navy of Britain might
ride in perfect security, let the wind blow
from any point of the compass. We came
to anchor about noon, and found a Portugueze snow laying here; she saluted
the Lion with eleven guns, which was
returned with nine. The captain came on

board, and informed us, the natives were
a little alarmed to see such a number of
ships, and some of so large a size, come
in; they wished to know from whence we
came, whither we were bound, and our
reasons for touching at Turon. All these
questions were answered in such a manner as to dissipate their fears. As soon
as the ships were moored, the old man
was sent on shore; his joy was then as
extravagant as his grief before had been;
but he did not refuse a couple of dollars
now, which had repeatedly been offered
to him before. We soon understood that
this country had been involved in war for
some years back, and that peace was only
just established; the particulars I could
not sufficiently understand, but that the
present king's father, who was tributary
to some neighbouring power, had raised
a formidable army, and by dint of courage
and perseverance, had established himself
firmly on the throne; he also subdued the

little kingdoms of Ava, Laos, and Siam;
it was said that above one hundred thousand souls had fallen a sacrifice to his
ambition; and he lived but just to finish
the bloody work he had begun, and left
a prince, about fourteen years of age,
under the guardianship of his uncle; this
prince they say is surrounded by numerous guards, regularly disciplined, and
trained to war: his capital is a considerable distance up the country. At the bottom of this bay there is a largish village,
or rather cluster of huts; it stands at the
entrance of a fine river. About twelve
miles farther up, there is a large town
called Fyfo, which used to be a place of
great trade, but now all communication
between this and the neighbouring states
is cut off; it is far from being of that consequence it used to be. The interior of
the country is very rich; it produceth vast
quantities of silver, which they used to
exchange for the produce of other places.

Their boats, swords, tobacco-pipes, and almost all their utensils, are plated with this desirable metal, and they have wedges of it continually about them. What we chiefly wanted with them was provisions. Several of the mandarins paid us a visit, and promised to let us have all we wanted, as speedily as it could be got down from the country. They invited our gentlemen to pay them a visit on shore, and the chief mandarin gave them a treat, which consisted of pork, goat, buffalo, rice, and fish, dressed in a variety of ways, so as to consist of near an hundred dishes. The chief inconvenience they experienced, was the want of knives or forks, in lieu of which they were obliged to make use of two small canes, and a shell supplied the use of a spoon. When they returned on board a very inconsiderable present was sent to his Lordship.

On the 29th tents were fixed, and the

G

sick sent on shore, for whom we were able to procure a few temporary necessaries, such as ducks, sugar, &c. &c. On the 2d of June the troops belonging to his Lordship's guard had their arms delivered to them, to be in readiness to attend him whenever he went on shore, and were all (sick and servants excepted) mustered on board the Lion, where they were to stop during the rest of the voyage. The 4th of June, being his Majesty's birthday, the Lion, Hindostan, and the Portugueze brig, each fired a royal salute. Lord Macartney and his suite went on shore, at the earnest request of the principal mandarin; the two brigs went to the mouth of the river the day before, and his Lordship had a party of fifty men, well armed, to guard him from any hostile attempt they might be induced to make; for we were not perfectly assured of their sincerity; nor would his Lordship have ventured amongst them, but in hopes his condescension would have a good effect, and induce them to send us a speedy supply, particularly for the sick, who were in great distress. The present his Lordship took ashore for the young Prince, was a fine double barrelled gun, a present of great value in this country, particularly the fire-arms, of which they are prodigiously fond. These people know the use of gunpowder well, but they have few muskets, and those few miserably bad.

The following day we received in return two buffaloes, a little rice, and a few ducks; the buffalo so miserably poor, that one we killed immediately could scarcely be eaten, and the other died two days after. On the 6th of June the tents on shore were all struck, and the sick removed on board; they were, in general, far better than on our arrival at this place, though many were still in a bad way, and the recovery of many of them doubtful. We had not been able to procure

them all the nourishment their different
ailments required, for during the three
weeks we lay here, we could get nothing
but a few ducks, a little fish, some sweet
potatoes, and sugar. The ducks were
pretty good, and after some time not un-
reasonable; but at first, the mercenary
rascals, seeing our eagerness to get them,
would only give us two for a dollar, afterwards three, and so on, as we became
careless about them, we could get ten or
twelve very fine ones. On Wednesday the
5th, the Jackall, with some of the gentlemen on board, went to take a survey of
some island and bay to the northward.
They found a fine town or village, which
from its appearance on going into the
harbour, they thought must have been
built either by Europeans or Chinese.
The houses were of stone, and regular.
On going ashore they found the natives
very busy in preparing immense quantities of mortar, and other materials, as if

a work of great magnitude was going to
be undertaken. As they advanced further
into the place, they found a number of
curious things, sufficient to excite their
astonishment, in such an uncouth country
as it appeared all around this little paradise.
They noticed most, a building of some
magnitude, supported in front on well polished pillars of marble, and ornamented
in different places with images, and Chinese characters, that would not have disgraced an European workman. The building was neither fantastically light, or
clumsy, and all around it there was a
spacious well laid out garden, with regular walks; and at a great distance as far
as the eye could reach, the country was
beautifully enriched with paddy fields in
a fine state of cultivation. Our gentry
of course paid greater attention than
ordinary to such a scene, and were highly
delighted with it. The natives seemed
jealous, and wished, though feared, to

interrupt them. They took a very accurate survey of the harbour, and all they thought worth notice, and endeavoured to learn what occasioned such a difference between these people and those around them. They resemble each other in person, in dress, and in many different customs, but they have many peculiarities which are no where else to be found. They found among them many pagodas, in which were the images they worshipped, richly decked out. They are amazingly superstitious in religious affairs, but not so grossly ignorant as the people at Turon, especially the lower class. The mandarins are sharp enough, and easily comprehend any thing you would explain to them. The young prince's uncle, a very intelligent man, desired one of our gentlemen to show him the globe, and point out his own country, as he was given to understand an Englishman knew and visited every part of it. His request was complied with, and he made a number of pointed remarks on the different countries shown to him; he at last desired they would let him see England, as no doubt, he said, it must be of considerable magnitude to furnish fleets and armies to every part of the world. They were ashamed to let him see so insignificant an island as it appeared to be; they therefore carried him from England and Ireland across the Atlantic, and pointed out a considerable part of America and the West India islands, as belonging to the king their master, whom they represented as the most powerful monarch upon the earth, and to whom many other kings and princes were tributary. The vast size of our ships, and the thunder of our 24 pounders, struck them with astonishment, and induced them at least to treat us with civility. Had our vessels been small and unarmed, I believe we should have come off scurvily amongst them; when those

in the Jackall had made their observations,
and were working out of the harbour
before mentioned, they observed twelve
very large proas, crowded with men, regularly ranged across the harbour's mouth,
evidently with a design to oppose their passage; not seeing any guns on board her,
they expected no resistance; but she had
several swivel guns, and were otherwise
well provided, and therefore pushed reso-
lutely forward, and made a proper disposition of their little force. When they came
pretty near, they fired one of their swivels
and a few muskets over their heads; this
had a wonderful effect, they directly opened
to the right and left, to make a passage,
and lay upon their oars, staring with
stupid wonder on the little brig, as she
passed through them, nor dared they to
offer her any molestation. She arrived
safe at Turon Bay the 7th of June. The
same day a boat from the Lion, in which
was the master and seven men, was sent

up this river to take a survey of it. For
fear of creating suspicion, they had strict
orders to go no higher than the mandarins should direct them; but venturing to
exceed a little the liberty given them,
they were all seized and thrown into pri-
son; their draughts and instruments were
also taken away. This affair created much
trouble to his Lordship and Sir Erasmus
Gower, not knowing how to proceed in
it; they censured the unwary conduct of
the officer; but being a subject of Great
Britain, and an officer in the navy, they
could not avoid demanding his restitution
in very pointed terms, threatening force,
if mild arguments were insufficient. At
the same time they desired the mandarins
to assure the prince, that his conduct had
no sanction from them, and that he would
be brought to a very strict account for his
disobedience of orders. Our boats went
on shore, as usual, to purchase provisions,
and met with no molestation, though the

mandarins were less frequent in their
visits on board than they used to be.
Before this happened, five or six large
boats would come to us every day, in
which were several of their chiefs, and
30 or 40 of their dependents. These
boats were very long and high at the
head and stern, like a Chinese junk, the
seats were raised very high, on which
mats were spread, and umbrellas fixed,
and on each side (if a mandarin of war)
about a dozen long spears, and other warlike instruments. Besides rowers, which
were from 12 to 40 in number, they had
generally five or six soldiers, with swords
slung over their shoulders. I got permission to examine one of them, which was
really a very capital weapon. It was something like our swords in shape, but stouter;
the hilt was the smaller end of an ele-
phant's tooth, and the scabbard was a kind
of hard wood, the colour of mahogany, elegantly polished, and covered in different

parts with plates of silver. The dress of
the chiefs was something in the Persian fashion, consisting of a pair of loose drawers,
and a long wide gown of dark cotton, but-
toned round their necks, very wide sleeves,
and flowing loosely down to their ancles;
over this some of them wore an upper gar-
ment of fine white flowered silk. Round
their heads they wear a long roll of dark
cotton or muslin, in the form of a turban.
They have a number of servants at their
heels, with umbrellas, pipes, tobacco, spit-
ting boxes, fans, &c. The dress of the
common sort of these people, was only a
pair of cotton drawers, reaching down to
the calf of their legs, and a turban like
those already described, only of inferior
stuff. In their boats they had a fine and
large reservoir of water, and different necessary utensils, and plenty of provisions.
Whenever they came alongside, and their
chiefs were on board, they squatted down
upon their heels like the Malays, each

with a bason full of boiled rice. They have two long pieces of cane, with which they shove in their victuals with wonderful activity. As soon as each has finished his meal, he washes himself, and lays down quietly to sleep under a matting. In many respects these people appear to be a mixture of Chinese and Malays. Their huts are but meanly built of bamboo: in the front of each there is a shed, supported by wooden pillars, underneath which, is a decent seat of cane, covered with matting, to repose themselves upon. The inside of the house is lined with pictures and characters in the Chinese style. The houses are small or large, which distinguishes the rank and quality of the owner, but all alike mean. In each town or village they have a larger building than ordinary, in which they transact all public business, and entertain strangers. It was one of these in which Lord Macartney was feasted, and entertained with a

kind of play, performed by young people
of both sexes, describing the warlike conduct of one of their chiefs, and accompanied with vocal and instrumental music,
but harsh and disagreeable. The women
cannot be distinguished from the men by
their dress; but they are more delicate, and
some of them, particularly the actresses,
are very handsome; but in general, they
smell rank, like the Malays. The domes-
tic animals are remarkably large, ele-
phants, a few horses, goats, and pigs; and
all the wild ones we saw were buffaloes
and monkies. They abound with fowls
and pelicans. I saw several fish; they
have plenty, which they are very fond of
when mixed with rice.

On the 10th of June, we had completed
our stock of water, and waited for nothing
but the men that were detained on shore
to put to sea; the next day was fixed upon
to sail, but the disagreeable affair detained

us, much to the vexation of every one
on board. The weather had been so very
sultry and unhealthy, that few of us but
were afflicted with one complaint or other.
On the 12th of June, Mr. Tottle, Purser
of the Lion, departed this life, and was
buried the same day near the watering
place.

On the 14th, the Master of the Lion,
men and boat, were all set at liberty, and
sent on board, with their drawings, and
every thing belonging to them. A very
handsome apology from the young Prince,
and a present of rice accompanied them.
On the 15th, we left Turon Bay, and on
the 20th came to an anchor amongst a cluster of large islands opposite the entrance
of Canton river. The same day, the two
brigs with Captain Mackintosh, Sir George
Staunton, and the two Chinese we brought
from England, all sailed for Macao. They
all returned except the two Chinese. On

the 22d, they brought along with them two French Jesuits who had been long resident in the country, and wanted a passage to Pekin. Early on the morning of the 23d, we got under sail with a fine stiff breeze. In the afternoon we spoke two Portugueze brigs going to Macao. This day George Martin, caulker's mate, departed this life, and his body was committed to the deep.

The 25th we had a heavy gale of wind, with thick hazy weather. The Lion and the Clarence both had their foretop-sails split, and their rigging much damaged. On the morning of the 26th, we passed the south-west end of the island of Formosa, but at a considerable distance; we could only just distinguish it, and it appeared very high land. In the evening, the Jackall had the misfortune to lose a man overboard, who fell from the yard arm as they were reefing topsails; it being dark, they could not possibly save him, though a good swimmer, and by the direction of his cries he survived some time, though the sea ran mountains high. On the 28th of June, the Lion separated, and left the two brigs in the Hindostan's charge, with the view of reaching Chusan more early, to overtake a Company's vessel which was stationed to cruize off that island for us till the 30th instant. The weather had been so hazy, and the wind so unsettled, that we could get no observation, and were doubtful if we could reach it in time to see her. On the 30th it cleared up, and blew pretty fresh from the south-west. On the 2d of July, we made the Bay of Chusan, and saw the Lion bearing down to us; she had been cruizing off the island for some time, but had not seen the vessel we expected. About noon, our little squadron came to an anchor in the bay. We were presently visited by several fishing boats, and saw

innumerable fleets of them all over the
bay. The same day the Clarence, with Sir
George Staunton and Captain Mackintosh,
sailed to the head of the bay to Chusan, a
very considerable place, to procure if possible, some tidings of the Company's vessel,
which probably must have been seen by
some of their boats; to see if they could
procure a pilot to carry us to Pekin.
During the time we lay here we had very
unsettled weather; the mornings generally were clear and pleasant, but towards
noon, it began to blow and rain with great
violence; but being in the latitude of 30
north, it was not so violently hot as we
had felt it for some months past: our
ship's crew recovered their health fast,
and we had but one or two dangerously
ill. The crew of the Lion remained in a
very sickly condition, and from the time
we anchored to the 6th of July, she buried
five seaman, and had sixty in the sur-
geon's list. We procured refreshments
H

here, as excellent fish, tea, sugar, &c.
cheap as we could wish it to be, and very
good. The number of junks, fishing boats,
and vessels of different sorts and sizes,
continually cruizing in this bay astonished
us all. At a very moderate computation,
I suppose we might see every day three
or four hundred, a chief part of them very
large; and the number of people on board
of them was still more surprising ; in the
smallest fishing boat they had generally
twelve hands. They had never seen any
vessels of such a size and construction as
ours before in these parts, and were very
curious in visiting the different parts of the
ship, and admired every thing they saw.
Several who first visited us returned, and
brought their fathers or relations to see
the wonders themselves had seen. Old
men, who apparently were almost deaf
and blind with age, waddled from deck
to deck with open mouths and uplifted
hands, admiring a sight so wonderfully

strange. Some mandarins of the third
rank, paid us a visit, and took dimensions
of the ship, masts, &c. &c. On the morning of the 7th, the Clarence returned and
brought us a pilot; and about noon, on
the 8th of July, we weighed anchor, having a stiff breeze from the north-east, and
a heavy swell from that quarter. Towards
dusk, we got quite clear of the land, and
stood out to sea all night, notwithstanding
the remonstrances of our Chinese pilot, who
wished very much to have the ship brought
to an anchor, or to keep within sight of
land. We had but very indifferent weather
till the 10th, when the wind got round more
favourable, and did not blow too hard. On
the evening of that day, we saw the island
of Cheu Teing Tong, bearing north-west
by north, distant eight leagues. Early
next morning, we saw several more
islands to the northward and westward,
and stood in towards land with a fine
steady breeze from the southward. We

were this day, in 30° 7′ north latitude,
and found the weather much more comfortable than it had been for many preceding months; the sick recovered fast,
and all hands were cheerful, in the pleasing hope of being, in a few days, at the
end of a tedious, troublesome, and disagreeable voyage. The 12th and 13th,
we had thick foggy weather and unsteady
winds, and lost sight of each other, notwithstanding we kept firing guns every
half hour, and were answered till about
12 o'clock at night. On the 14th, when
we supposed they must all have altered
their course, it cleared up early in the
morning, and we discovered several vessels; they all proved to be Chinese junks,
except one, which was a brig under British colours; and to our unspeakable satisfaction, proved to be the Endeavour,
Captain Proctor, the vessel which was
fitted out by the East India Company to
cruize for us off the island of Chusan,

and to pilot us to the nearest port to Pekin. She had been, after leaving Chusan, to Teing Ching, and not finding us there, had been cruizing at the mouth of the Yellow sea, where we could not well enter without discovering each other; besides experienced pilots, she had on board one or more interpreters, without whom, we should have been placed in an awkward situation on our arrival. The wind, this day, proving favourable and pretty fresh, we had a prospect of reaching our destined port in two or three days more: all that we wished for now, to render our satisfaction complete, was a sight of our other ships; and we fell in with them on the morning of the 16th, off the northernmost extremity of the coast of China. We had mistaken their signal guns in the foggy night we parted from them, and they had passed ahead of us, owing to our mistake. On the 17th, we were abreast of the northern point, which is

in about 38° north latitude. The Endeavour was far astern, and was so bad a
sailer, that we could not keep her company if we carried any canvas at all.
Being also so near our port, and having
a very distinct view of the land, we were
not so anxious about her as we had formerly been. We had taken the inter-
preter out of her, and given the Captain
proper directions where to follow us, to
receive further instructions from his Lordship. During the time of our separation,
we had but very indifferent weather, generally thick and foggy. Our soundings
were pretty regular from 8 to 30 fathoms,
as we approached, or left the land. The
Yellow sea (or river) was here not more
than 30 leagues wide. We could, when
the weather was clear, plainly distinguish the coast of China on one side,
and the land of Mozea on the other. We
in general, kept pretty close to the former,
that we might make our pilot useful, as

he seemed pretty well acquainted with
the land; but out of sight of it, he was
entirely useless. The 18th proved thick
and dirty, with easy variable winds. We
had got round the westward into the bay.
Several very large junks were in sight,
from one of which we got another pilot.
The 19th was as the day preceding; so
thick and foggy, that we were obliged to
keep firing guns to prevent another separation. As we could not see the land, we
lay too with our larboard tacks aboard;
and the ships could not be seen through
the fog, though their guns could be heard
very distinctly. About eight in the morning, the Jackall ran under our stern, and
informed us we were close in with the land,
which bore from east to south-south-west
from us, and that she had run within three
quarters of a mile of it before she had
perceived it; and wished for instruction
what course to steer. About an hour
after, the sun broke through, and entirely

dispelled the mist, so that we had a perfect view of our little fleet, and the land too. A fine breeze from the eastward bore us away before it; and we had a pleasing hope of coming to an anchor before the evening. The land was rather low on the coast, but seemed hilly in the back ground. All apparently finely cultivated, and well inhabited. Many large junks were in sight all day. Towards evening, we stood into a fine large bay, which we mistook for Mataw; a place of some such name, where we had appointed Captain Proctor, in the Endeavour, to join us, in case of separation. We passed very near the shore, and could plainly perceive the inhabitants crowding upon the hills to see us, and running to and fro, as in great amazement. We anchored before sunset; and had a boat from shore presently, by which we soon understood our mistake, and learnt that we were 10 leagues to the south-east of our intended port.

On the 20th of July, we got up our anchor, and passed through several pleasant islands. We distinguished the houses scattered about along the beach, in delightful rural situations; and every inch of ground seemed in a high state of cultivation, except the very summit of the rocks. We saw a town of some note, and several large junks at anchor near it; and as we passed along, the most delightful prospects presented themselves we ever saw. Houses scattered here and there, all over a most extensive valley, villages, and larger towns, at the distance of about a mile from each other, in a country beautiful beyond description. About six o'clock in the evening, we anchored in an open bay, opposite on one side to Mataw, and on the other to the city of Teing Chew. This city is entirely walled round; and as we judged about 16 miles in circumference. Its being situated on a rising ground, gave

us a view of the walls almost all round;
and enabled us to form a pretty exact
idea of its extent. The walls are built of
stone, and were so high, that we could
only see a few houses on the rise of the
hills ; and the walls were, I believe, thick
in proportion; for as we came in, we could,
with the help of our glasses, see hundreds
of people gathered in crowds, upon that
part of the wall nearest the shore, to gaze
at us. At about the distance of an hundred yards, there were round towers of a
considerable height ; and at the northern
extremity of the city, there seemed to be
a pretty strong battery, with several cannon mounted upon it. Round about the
walls on the outside, were tents pitched,
we supposed for the military. We had
several boats came off to us, but they
only brought a few fish. This harbour
lay, by observation, in about 38° north
latitude.

On Monday July 22d, the Endeavour brig, Captain Proctor arrived, and saluted the Lion with six guns, which was returned with four; the Jackall was dispatched to sound the bar and harbour of Tsing Ching; this harbour being judged unsafe for the shipping, if a gale of wind should come on. About noon we got a pilot on board, and weighed anchor for Tsing Ching. This day, bombardier M'Intire, of the Royal Artillery, died on board of the Lion: his death was occasioned by a flux, with which several others of his Lordship's guard were afflicted. An order from Lord Macartney, was this day read to the troops on board of the Lion, to the following effect:

MACARTNEY. (Copy.)

" As the ships and brigs attendant upon the Embassy to China, are now likely to arrive in port there a few days hence,

his Excellency the Embassador, thinks it
his duty to make the following observations and arrangements :—It is impossible
that the various and important objects of
the Embassy can be obtained, but through
the good will of the Chinese; this good
will may much depend on the ideas which
they shall be induced to entertain of the
disposition and conduct of the English
nation. They can judge only from the
behaviour of those who come amongst
them. It must be confessed that the impressions hitherto made upon their minds,
in consequence of the irregularities committed by Englishmen at Canton, are
unfavourable, even to the degree of considering them as the worst of Europeans.
These impressions are communicated in
course to that tribunal, in the capital,
which reports to, and advises the Emperor upon all concerns with foreign
countries. It is therefore essential, by a
conduct particularly regular and circum-

spect, to impress them with new, just, and more favourable ideas of Englishmen; and to shew that even to the lowest officer in the sea or land service, or in the civil line, they are capable of maintaining, by example and by discipline, due order, sobriety, and subordination among their respective inferiors. The people in China have not the smallest share in the government, yet it is a maxim invariably pursued by their superiors, to support the meanest Chinese in any difference with a stranger; and, if the occasion should happen, to avenge his blood, of which indeed there was a fatal instance not long since at Canton, where the gunner of an English vessel, who had been very innocently the cause of the death of a native peasant, was executed for it, notwithstanding the united efforts, on the part of the several European factories at Canton, to save him. Peculiar caution and mildness must consequently be observed in every sort of intercourse or accidental meeting, with any the poorest individuals of the country.

" His Excellency, who well knows that he need not recommend to Sir Erasmus Gower to make whatever regulations prudence may dictate on this occasion for the persons under his immediate command; as he hopes Captain Mackintosh will do for the officers and crew of the Hindostan. He trusts also, that the propriety and necessity of such regulations, calculated to preserve the credit of the English name, and the interest of the mother country in these remote parts, will insure a steady and cheerful obedience.

" The same motives, he flatters himself, will likewise operate upon all the persons immediately connected with, or in the service of the Embassy. His Excellency declares, that as he shall be ready to encourage, and to report favourably home upon the good conduct of those who shall be found to deserve it; so he will think it his duty, in case of misconduct or disobedience of orders, to report the same with equal exactness, and to suspend or dismiss transgressors, as the occasion may require. Nor, if any offence should be offered to a Chinese, or a misdemeanor of any kind be committed, which may be punishable by their laws, will he deem himself bound to interfere, for the purpose of endeavouring to ward off, or mitigate their severity. His Excellency relies upon Lieutenant-Colonel Benson, commandant of his guard, that he will have a strict and watchful eye over them. Vigilance, as to their personal demeanor, is as requisite in the present circumstances, as it is, though from other motives, in regard to the conduct of an enemy in time of war. The guard are to be kept constantly together, and regularly

exercised in all military evolutions; nor
are any of them to absent themselves
from on board ship; or from whatever
place may be allotted them for their dwelling on shore, without leave from his Excellency, or commanding officer. None
of the mechanics or servants are to leave
the ship, or usual dwelling on shore, without leave from himself or Mr. Maxwell;
and his Excellency expects, that the gentlemen in his train will show the example
of subordination, by communicating their
wishes to him, before they go on any occasion from the ship, or usual dwelling
place on shore. No boxes, or packages
of any kind, are to be removed from the
ship, or afterwards from the place where
they shall be brought on shore, without
the Embassador's leave, or a written order
from Mr. Barlow, the comptroller; such
order describing the nature, number, and
dimension of such package. His Excellency, in the most earnest manner,

requests that no person whatever belonging to the ships be suffered, and he desires that none of his suite, guard, mechanics, or servants, presume to offer for sale, or propose to purchase, in the way of traffic, the smallest article of merchandize of any kind, or under any pretence whatever, without leave from him previously obtained. The necessity of avoiding the least appearance of traffic accompanying an Embassy to Pekin, was such as to induce the East India Company to forego the profits of a new market; and deterred them from shipping any goods for sale in the Hindostan, as being destined to attend upon the Embassy; the dignity and importance of which, in the prejudiced eyes of the Chinese, would be utterly lost, and the good consequences expected from it on commercial points totally prevented, if any actual transactions, though for trifles for the purpose of gain, should be disco-

I

vered amongst any of the persons concerned in conveying, or attending an
Ambassador, of which the report would
soon infallibly swell into a general sys-
tem of trading. From this strictness his
Excellency will willingly relax, whenever
such advances shall have been made by
him in negotiation, as will secure the
object of his mission; and when a permission from him to an European to dispose of any particular article of merchandize, shall be considered as a favour granted
to the Chinese purchaser.

" His Excellency is bound to punish, as
far as in him lies, any deviation from
this regulation; he will easily have it in
his power to do so, in regard to the persons
immediately in his train or service: the
discipline of the navy will render it equally easy to Sir Erasmus Gower, in respect
to those under his immediate command;
and the East India Company have by

their order of the 5th of September, 1792,
and by their letter of the 8th of the same
month and year, fully authorized his Excellency to enforce compliance with the
same regulations among the officers of
the Hindostan. A copy of the said order, and an extract from the said letters,
here follow, in order that Captain Mackintosh may communicate the same to his
officers : and his Excellency depends upon
him to prevent any breach or evasion of
the same, among any of his crew.

" At a Court of Directors held on Wed-
" nesday, the 5th of September, 1792 :

" Resolved, that the Right Honourable
Lord Viscount Macartney be authorized
to suspend or dismiss the commander,
or any officers of the Hindostan, who
shall be guilty of a breach of covenants
or disobedience of orders from the Secret Committee, or from his Excellency,

during the continuation of the Embassy
to China.

  (Signed) W. RAMSAY, Sec."

 " Extract from the Chairman and De-
puty Chairman's Letter to Lord Macartney, dated September 8, 1792.

 " The Secret Committee have given
orders to Captain Mackintosh, of the
Hindostan, to put himself entirely under
your Excellency's direction, so long as
may be necessary for the purpose of the
Embassy. We have inclosed a copy of
his instructions, and of the covenant
which he has entered into, together with
an account of his private trade and that
of his officers. There is no intention
whatever, on the part of the Court, to
permit private trade in any other port or
place than Canton, to which the ship is
ultimately destined, unless your Excellency is satisfied, that such private trade

will not prove of detriment to the dignity
and importance annexed to the Embassy,
or to the consequences expected there-
from ; in which case, your consent in
writing becomes necessary, to authorize
any commercial transactions by Captain
Mackintosh, or any of his officers, as explained in the instructions from the Secret
Committee. But, as we cannot be too
guarded with respect to trade, and the
consequences which may result for that
purpose, we hereby authorize your Excellency to suspend, or dismiss the commander, or any officers of the Hindostan,
who shall be guilty of a breach of covenants, or disobedience of orders from the
Secret Committee, or from your Excellency, during the continuation of the present
Embassy."

" His Excellency takes this opportunity
of declaring also, that however determined
his sense of duty makes him, to forward

the objects of his mission, and to watch, detect, and punish, as far as in his power, any crime, disobedience of orders, or other behaviour, tending to endanger or delay the success of the present undertaking, or to bring discredit on the English character, or occasion any difficulty or embarrassment to the Embassy: so in like manner shall he feel himself happy, in being able at all times to report and reward the merit, as well as to promote the interest, and indulge the wishes, of every person who has accompanied him on this occasion, as much as may be, consistent with the honour and welfare of the public.

" In case of the absence or engagements of his Excellency, at any particular moment, applications may be made in his room to Sir George Staunton, whom his Majesty was pleased to honour with a commission of Minister Plenipotentiary, to act on such occasions.

"Given on board his Majesty's ship the,
Lion, this 16th day of July, 1793.

By his Excellency's command.

(Signed)   ACHESON MAXWELL,
           EDWARD WINDER,
               Secretaries."

On Tuesday the 23d of July, Redford,
of the Royal Artillery, departed this life,
and was committed to the deep the same
evening. On Wednesday, we were nearly
becalmed all day. In the evening, the
Jackall made a signal for land ahead, and
presently after fired three guns to warn
us of our danger. On sounding, we had
only 7 fathoms water: we immediately
put the ship about, and stood away till
daylight on Thursday, when we stood in
again for land. About 10 o'clock, we discovered a low sandy island, behind which
were a great number of Chinese junks
riding at anchor. We had this day, only
from 12 to 5 fathoms of water, though

entirely out of sight of land, excepting
that small island before mentioned, and
were obliged to anchor in the evening,
opposite Ching Ching, without being able
to see any land, except from the mast
head. We were not more than 15 or 20
miles at the utmost from the mouth of the
river, but the land being so low, was the
reason we could not see it. The Jackall
joined us the following day, and gave us
a very unsatisfactory account: she could
not find water sufficient for us, nor even
for herself, to lay with safety. She had
been aground three times, and lost an
anchor in the attempt. The Endeavour,
Captain Proctor, was then dispatched to
see what she could do, as she had a less
draught of water, and had either been
here before or mistaken the bay, for at the
time we first spoke her, she told us she
had been in here after us, and that there
was room and water sufficient for any
number or size of shipping.

On Friday the 26th a large junk, having on board some mandarins of the first and second rank, came to us, and told his Lordship, that proper vessels were getting ready to convey his Excellency, suite, and baggage on shore, or up to Pekin; and that we might daily expect them to come off to us : we were, therefore, all busied in preparing to disembark; and most heartily and cheerfully did we all exert ourselves on so pleasing a piece of business; seamen and others, the former being as anxious to get back to Chusan or Canton, as we were to be, once more, on terra firma. The officers and others belonging to the ships, were much disappointed, and not a little mortified, at not being able to see the so much famed capital of China. This open bay being too wide for the vessels to lay in safety, it was determined they should return to one of the before-mentioned places, with as much speed as

possible, after landing every thing destined for Pekin.

Monday, July the 29th, another large
Chinese junk paid us a visit, and brought
with her a present of fresh provisions and
fruit for his Lordship; part of which was
sent to the gentlemen on board the Hindostan.   She informed us, the vessels before mentioned, were getting ready with
all convenient speed, and that they probably would be with us the following day.
The 30th, in the afternoon, the Endeavour hove in sight; and on the 31st, a
considerable number of junks appeared
astern of us; but having wind and tide
unfavourable, they were obliged to anchor
to leeward, about 12 miles.   The Endeavour came too, at noon, under our stern :
by her we understood, the junks were
those so long and so eagerly expected by
us. Early this morning, John Kay, joiner

and cabinet-maker, of the Hindostan, died, after a lingering illness of ten months; his body was committed to the deep in the usual manner.

August the 2d, some of the junks came alongside, and took in several things belonging to his Lordship and the Embassy : and on the evening of the 3d, they had nearly completed taking every thing from the shipping that was intended to go ashore ; and the troops received orders to hold themselves in readiness, to disembark at a moment's notice. On the 4th, they went on board the junks, and got into the mouth of the river. The following afternoon, his Lordship was saluted with 19 guns from each ship, on his disembarkation. The three brigs accompanied us into the river; and stopped with us, till we got on board some accommodation boats, which were provided to carry us up the river. These boats were the

most convenient and commodious that can
possibly be conceived; they are broad and
flat bottomed; and the smallest draught
of water is sufficient, though they will
carry a surprising weight of goods. On
the deck, they have a kind of house, consisting of a variety of different apartments
for sleeping, eating, cooking, &c. all
finished in a capital style. We had upwards of 20 of these vessels, of different
constructions, provided for us; and every
attention paid that could possibly be expected, to render our passage up to the
capital easy and comfortable. From the
chief mandarins to the poorest peasant,
all seemed anxious to convince us we
were welcome: indeed it was as great a
novelty to them as it was to us; and, if
we were entertained with them and their
droll appearances, they were not less delighted with ours; and we strove, by every
art we were master of, to excite their
wonder and amazement. On Friday

the 9th of August, having every thing
regulated to our satisfaction, we proceeded up the river; there were some mandarins appointed to go along with us, to see
that provisions and every thing necessary,
were ready whenever we stopped. The
two first days, we got up about 40 English miles, on the most delightful river I
ever beheld; the Thames itself, in my
opinion, does not exceed it, except in the
variety of its prospects. This river, was
nearly as wide as the Thames at Ham-
mersmith or Kew; and continued, without any perceivable difference, or branch-
ing off, nearly the same. On each side
were towns and villages, scarcely the
distance of a mile apart, and the shores
covered with multitudes of the natives,
who crowded down to see us pass. The
prospect was not various or extensive, the
country being so low, but every inch of
ground seemed cultivated in the highest
style. On the third day, the country

presented a more enlivening prospect, and charming beyond description. I had formed an idea of it before our landing, not unfavourable to the Chinese; but, I confess, this exceeded my utmost expectation, in every point of view. We arrived early this day, at the city Tien Sing, where a sumptuous entertainment was provided for his Lordship, and the gentlemen in his train; and a very handsome cold collation of fowls, fruit, &c. sent to his attendants and guard, on board their respective boats; which were all drawn up in such a manner, that they had a full view of a musical tragi-comic representation, in the Chinese style; performed in a temporary building, erected for that purpose, in the front of the chief mandarin's house. The performers were numerous, richly dressed, and very active in different ludicrous attitudes they put themselves into. This entertainment lasted about three hours; and when it was

finished, the boats began to move slowly
forward. Upon a moderate calculation,
the concourse of people gathered together, was supposed to amount to two
millions; the houses and vessels were
scarcely perceivable for them; and hundreds of them waded up to their necks in
water, to gain a sight of us, as we went
along. On one side of the river were
several regiments of soldiers drawn up
under arms; some with bows and arrows;
others with miserable matchlocks; and
some with shields and spears. They were
all nearly in the same uniform; and what
appeared so laughable and singular to our
troops was, that very few of them were
without a pipe in his mouth, and a fan in
his hand, to cool and shield him from the
sun; and as we passed along, we found
very few without either; and what was
more surprising, great numbers of them
setting down in the ranks; they were
not particular to a yard or two, in dress-

ing their rank, nor in what form they
sit or stand; but their distances pretty
regularly about three paces each. Every
third man carries small colours; the staff
of which is stuck in his clothes, behind
the neck, and is about two feet above his
head, so as not to encumber his hand:
and about every twelfth man, there is a
large standard, which is under the care of
two men; one in front, the other in the
rear, unarmed: their dress put me in mind
of a mountebank's fool's dress, though I
dare say, very serviceable in the time of
action; it consists of a helmet of steel,
and made in such a manner that it would
shelter the head against any cut; it comes
down to the brow and neck; it is round,
and comes off taper to the top; on which
is fixed a kind of spear, about a foot long,
ornamented with red horse hair, hanging
down. Their jacket, or what they wear
instead, is really frightful at a distance;
it is beset with thin pieces of iron or brass,

which imitates an English brass nailed
trunk; and it is made to cover that part
of the neck which the helmet leaves uncovered, and buttons to it on each side,
and meets itself above the mouth, so that
no parts of the head or face are exposed, but
just the eyes.

The chief mandarin at Tien Sing, made
a very handsome present of silks, &c. to
all the gentlemen, servants, and soldiers
in his Lordship's train. The following five
or six days, the prospects on each side began to be more variegated and delightful :
the country was seen to a great distance,
and the hills which divide China from
Tartary, could be very distinctly seen.
The seats of the mandarins were scattered
here and there, surrounded by tufts of evergreens, and the villages interspersed, formed a most charming rural prospect. The
shores of the river were lined with the natives on each side, who had got together

K

from curiosity, or to dispose of their fruits, &c. which we were able to purchase in great plenty, and tolerably reasonable; such as apples, water and mesh melons, peaches, apricots, &c. What surprised us much was, that the women appeared to be under as little restraint here as in England, as we had been told, it was very rare to gain a sight of any female in China, they not being allowed to leave the house, except in covered chairs or carriages, where no one could see them; but thus far, we saw them near every house or village, though not quite in number proportionable to the other sex. I believe it is reckoned a disgrace to have many female children; a boy gives more pleasure at his birth to his parents, and is taken care of; but the girls are cruelly neglected by their parents; they are frequently suffered to perish through want, or wilfully thrown into a neighbouring river, without the least remorse, or any notice being taken of it by

those whose duty we think it is to punish
such inhumanity: pity has sometimes induced those of ample fortunes, to rescue a
few of these poor infants from such an
early and untimely death, and to bring
them up comfortably, without making any
inquiry from whom they came: but instances of this kind are very rare; and I
was told the practice itself, of exposing
their infants to perish, is wearing away
very fast. After an inland voyage of about
an hundred miles, on Saturday the 17th,
we landed at Tong Chew, a city about 12
miles from Pekin. The crowds of people
gathered together to see us land were astonishing; it required the utmost exertions
of a great number of the military, to keep
them from absolutely smothering of us; it
was not possible even for an English soldier to go along the streets for some days,
without having a native soldier along with
him to clear the way with a whip, which
they carry for that purpose; and which

they sometimes use very unmercifully, upon the bare backs of the inhabitants.

We met with great hospitality and respect from all ranks of people during our stay here, and had very comfortable accommodations, with regard to lodgings and provisions. At this place we buried a mechanic belonging to his Lordship, named Eades, a button-maker : and after a stay of four days, we departed on the 21st, at daybreak, in a kind of covered waggons and carts, which were the best carriages the country afforded, and such as the gentry use in travelling through the empire. I can compare them to nothing more like than the light country carts, without springs, used near London ; some covered with blue nankeen, others with fine bamboo matting. A very comfortable double mattress, covered with fine blue calico, is spread on the bottom of the best carriages, on which five or six Chinese will squat

down like so many tailors, though we
found it difficult to stow more than two,
and in the largest only three persons.
They use mules and asses to their carriages, the former of which, are remarkably large and strong. We entered the
celebrated city of Pekin early in the fore-
noon, but had no opportunity of seeing any
thing, except immense crowds of people on
each side of us, owing to the closeness of
the carriages in which we were confined;
all we could observe was, the walls, which
were very high and strong, built of large
bricks; and the houses were very low, and
rather shabby, of the same materials. But
probably those we saw were the outskirts,
and not so sumptuous as the interior parts
of the city. We had been induced to form
so high an idea of its amazing grandeur,
that I confess, we were somewhat disappointed; but no estimation could be formed from the little we saw. From gate
to gate, the distance we passed was five

or six miles : we then entered the suburbs,
which the Chinese inhabit, as the Tartars
do the city. The buildings here were truly
elegant, and the shops of the tradesmen
well stocked with all kinds of goods.
About noon, we were set down at a country seat belonging to the Emperor, six
miles to the northward of the city, called
Yuen-meng-yuen, where comfortable provision was made for us in every respect,
and where we had hopes to rest some considerable time : the general report which
prevailed amongst us was, that his Lordship, after a stay of ten days, would go on
to Tartary, by the Emperor's own appoint-
ment, and leave here only the mechanics
and the sick. This place was walled round,
and might be near 2 miles in extent, and
contained a vast variety of elegant little
buildings ; in the front of most of them
was a large canal for bathing, and other
useful purposes. The houses, or barracks
appointed for the guard, were in the middle

of a thick wood, but sufficiently open and airy, and surrounded with water; nothing, in short, could be more charming and delightful; or scarcely any thing exceed our vexation, when in about five or six days, we were ordered to get ready to return to Pekin, which we re-entered on the 26th, in the same manner we had passed through before, and were shut up like so many prisoners, amongst a large assemblage of buildings, walled round, and from which, we were not suffered to depart, nor even to take a peep over the walls. Some few, prompted by curiosity, ventured the latter, but being observed by the soldiers on the outside, a terrible clamour was instantly raised about our ears: 'The Place,' as it was named, in which we were, was in a few minutes filled with mandarins, and threatenings thundered out against any future transgressors. 'The Place' contained above fifty different buildings apart from each other, divided by large paved courts, be-

sides summer-houses, servants' apartments,
storehouses, and cooking shops an amazing number. Some of the buildings were
very regular, and neatly painted in the
Chinese fashion ; the outside displayed
much more elegance than the inside, which
contained no ornaments of any kind, sav-
ing a large vulgar painting at each end of
the room, nor any furniture, but a table,
and a matting for the floor. At one end
of the sleeping room, a bench is raised
about two feet from the floor, on this a
coarse woollen cloth and a mat is spread,
and for any other bedding or furniture,
you must find it yourself. We found many
inconveniences at first setting out, in this
new way of life, but custom soon recon-
ciled us, in a great measure, to their manners. In cooking, they appeared very awkward ; all their meat and vegetables being
hashed up in such a medley confusion, that
we scarcely knew at times what we were
eating ; but in great profusion: and in a

little time we brought them into a method of dressing our victuals, a little in the English way. Beef, mutton, and pork were excellent, as were their vegetables, such as sweet potatoes, cabbages, pumpkins, onions, and a great variety of others, common to both Europe and Asia. Fowls were also in great plenty, and excellent; but fish here was very uncommon. All their dishes are hashed or boiled; they have not the least notion of any other method of preparing them; but their soups are excellent. They eat but little bread; what they prepared for us was tolerably good; it was made into small round loaves or cakes, done in the steam, upon a kind of gridiron, and very light pleasant eating, when toasted afterwards. All our meals were regularly served, and a stated number of dishes to each table, one exactly the same as another, both meat, bread, and vegetables; and mandarins appointed to see every thing done in exact order, to prevent impositions, or any thing from being kept back, which were designed us; and in fact, this precaution was very necessary, for otherwise we should have been half starved. The lower class of Chinese, who are chiefly slaves, being the most thievish set of villains on the face of the earth; and withal so dexterous, that it was impossible to guard against them. It was a very common practice, on our first arrival, to keep back one half of our bread, sugar, tea, and sometimes whole pieces of meat; but after detection and the bastinado, they were more closely watched, and we fared sumptuously. They were not induced to rob us through want; had that been the case, we might have overlooked their impudence, but the meanest of them had a superfluity of the best provisions: it was disposed of, for a third of its value, to those people who originally sent it to us, and perhaps served in a different manner the next day, at our own table. The mandarins and people of better order, treated us with singular marks of attention and politeness, and were ever anxious to do us some acceptable piece of service, where it did not endanger their own personal safety; but the slightest deviation from any given order is punished with such severity, without regard to the rank of the offender, that all are very cautious; and more particularly, when that order respects any Europeans or strangers, of whom they are so unaccountably suspicious and fearful. It is true, we could boast of some indulgences never before granted to Europeans; but notwithstanding this, a restraint to which we had not been accustomed was unpleasant: for instance, his Lordship excepted, none of his train, gentle or simple, were ever allowed to leave the place appointed for them, not even to peep out of it, till permission was obtained; which generally created so much trouble, that they dropped their application, and patiently waited the issue, or looked forward to the time of a general enlargement.

On the 2d of September, his Excellency, attended by most of the gentry, servants, and guard, set off to pass, as a private visit, to the Emperor in Tartary. In the evening, they halted at a house of the Emperor's, about 22 miles from Pekin, called Mi-yuen-suen. On the 3d, we entered the hilly country, and a road as rough as could possibly be; and after a fatiguing journey of sixteen miles, were quartered in a large garrisoned town, just on the borders of Tartary. The following morning, we had a delightful view of the great wall, which divides that country from China. All were anxious to see this stupendous piece of ancient architecture, which had stood for so many ages the wonder of the world. By all accounts we could collect on the spot, and from the best informed Chinese, this wall was built near 1500 years ago, to prevent the incursions of the Tartars, who frequently made dreadful ravages, and plundered their northern provinces before any force could be collected to stop them. This wall, by report, extends in length, about 1400 miles; in general over an irregular mountainous country; and in many places over rocks and precipices, so dreadful in themselves, that one could not think any prospect of gain could induce men to venture their lives in passing them. That part of it which we measured and examined, with uncommon pains, was in height 25 feet, and in breadth, through the gate, 36 regular paces, which breadth it carried to the summit. In the vallies, both heighth and breadth far exceeded this account, or in other places, where the passage was open and exposed to danger. It was built of brick; many pieces of which were as anxiously collected as if they were wedges of the most precious metal, by all ranks, from his Excellency to the private soldier;

and though so ancient, yet in general, in
good order : some parts of it shows signs
of decay; nor is so much regard paid to
repair it since the union of the two empires.
At each gate there is a guard-house, where
some companies of soldiers are constantly
stationed ; and others are encamped at regular distances on each side of the wall.
The towers, on the top of it are at the distance of a musket shot from each other,
and from their astonishing bulk and height,
afford a prospect so extensive and magnificent, that imagination can form no idea
of it. From hence, we had four days' journey in Tartary, over hills and mountains,
and through vallies not unpleasant, but
very fatiguing, as we were often obliged
to leave the carriages in climbing and de-
scending the hills. The country appeared
fertile, though so rugged, and afforded
good pasturage for immense herds of sheep
and bullocks. It was but thinly peopled;
here and there a few scattered houses in

the vallies, but no place of note till we entered Gehor, on the 4th day, which was in the following order;—first, the light dragoons; then the royal artillery and infantry, all in slow march; next came the band of music, playing God save the King; they were followed by the gentlemen of the Embassy; the mechanics and servants brought up the rear. The place allotted for our reception, was just at the entrance of Gehor; at the gate of it, all were regularly drawn up, and saluted his Excellency as he entered, who was pleased to return his thanks, in a public manner, to the military, for the regularity and good order observed by them during the whole march and procession. Early on the morning of the 14th of September, the day appointed for delivering some of the presents from his Britannic Majesty to the Emperor, we all marched through Gehor (a town about 3 miles in extent,) to the Palace, in the above order; the presents in front of

the guard; but none, except his Excellency
and the gentlemen, were suffered to enter
the gates; all the others returned mortified
and terribly disappointed, as they had promised themselves great things from a sight
of this favourite and famous residence of
the greatest monarch on earth; nor could
they forbear indulging hopes of seeing his
Imperial Highness, in both which, they
were disappointed. However, they were in
some measure satisfied from a gratification
the outside afforded; the extent and elegance of it was beyond description, and
contrasted with the adjacent mountains
and precipices, the scene was great and
beautiful indeed, to which the rising sun
added a splendour truly magnificent. His
Excellency, during our stay at Gehor, had
four interviews with the Emperor, and was
received with most extraordinary honours;
and elegant presents each time was sent to
all his train, on their return to their own
quarters. An unaccountable number of

soldiers composed the Emperor's guard;
they were chiefly horsemen, and amount-
ed, by a moderate computation, to at least
twenty thousand.

On the 21st of September, we began
our journey back to Pekin, and the same
day had the misfortune to lose an artillery-
man, named Jeremiah Read; who was
buried the following day at Kola-choa-yen;
the whole of the detachment attending the
funeral. The flux, of which he died, had
by this time crept among us in a most
alarming manner; near half his Lordship's
guard were afflicted with it, and in a very
dangerous way The 23d, we arrived at
Kou-pee-keow, the pass through the great
wall from Eastern Tartary into China;
and on the 26th, once more re-entered
Pekin. The roads in China have been
reckoned the finest in the universe, and in
general they deserve that title; that in particular from Tartary into China, exceeds

L

every thing of the kind, I believe, in the world : it was made for the Emperor, on his return to his capital, and employed some thousand people, who keep it in constant repair, and are as a guard to it. No one but the Emperor is allowed to tread upon it. It is levelled every day, and I may add, every minute of the day; and is as level as a bowling-green. At the distance of an hundred yards from each other, cisterns are erected, to water it on the least appearance of dust. On each side, fine full grown poplars shade travellers from the scorching heat of the sun; as are also by the side of the road for the commonalty, which runs alongside the Emperor's road, and likewise upon every great road in the empire; and whenever a river, or small rivulet, crossed the Emperor's road, a most sumptuous bridge was erected; and to deaden the noise of the carriage wheels, the bottom was covered with fine matting. The posts, which supported the bridge, and the ornaments, which were numerous, and displayed with great ingenuity, were finely painted in various figures round about it.

On the 28th of September, Lord Macartney, attended by his suite, and a detachment of his guard, set off to meet the Emperor, at his palace near Yuen-ming-yuen, about 8 miles from Pekin; where, after the usual ceremonials, they left him, and arrived here again on the 29th. Some of the principal presents were deposited at this palace, which is the Emperor's favourite place of residence. The royal artillery delivered their guns a few days before, to be fixed here, viz. 4 one-pounders, 2 three-pounders, 2 twelve-inch howitzers, with a large supply of ammunition, &c. &c. &c. The Chinese are naturally such timid cowardly fellows, that it is a question if they ever make any use of them; indeed the very sight of these pieces strike them with terror, and the report will immediately drive them to a considerable distance, like so many frighted sheep.

October the 3d, a very handsome present was sent from the Emperor to his Lordship, the gentlemen in his suite, to the mechanics, servants, and guard; consisting of silk, tea, calico, and a variety of other things; besides several bars of virgin silver to the gentlemen, and one to each soldier, &c. &c. worth about three pounds sterling. This was a strong indication, that we were on the eve of our departure from Pekin; notwithstanding at our first entrance, we fully expected to winter there, and every individual among us was looking forward, with anxious expectation, to the grand audience between the Emperor and his Lordship: but we were soon given to understand, that the business of the Embassy had been finally adjusted at the last private meeting between them, at the Palace near Yuen-ming-yuen; that it was to the satisfaction of each, there was no doubt, or that the Emperor had agreed to every proposal from his Britannic Majesty, and the East India Company; but a profound secrecy was observed on the part of his Lordship.

The gentlemen in his suite seemed very much dissatisfied, that they were kept so much in the dark respecting it; and it was observed, that a general misunderstanding seemed breeding amongst them: some were pleased, and others were displeased, when on the 4th of October, an order was delivered for all to hold themselves in readiness to depart on the 7th.

We had all along been confined like so many prisoners, being never suffered to see any part of the city, nor to purchase any of the curiosities it contained, to carry to our friends in Europe. The unaccountable jealousy, and strange conduct of the Chinese, surprised us very much; though, in many instances, they treated us with singular marks of respect, yet all their attention to us seemed tempered with fear and dread; and it was apparent enough that they wished us away from amongst them, at least from their much famed capital, where no Europeans are suffered to go at large, except a few Jesuits; and they must conform to the Chinese dress, manners, and customs; nor are they allowed ever after to leave the empire, but are considered as subjects belonging to it; over them a particularly watchful eye is kept, lest they should steal away privately. But they seem very well satisfied with their lot; they live on the fat of the land, as most priests love to do, and have no laborious function to attend to. October the 6th, Henry Newman, of the royal artillery, departed this life; he was the sixth person of his Lordship's guard that we had lost already, and several others were in a de-

spairing way. On the 7th we took a final
leave of Pekin; we were in open carriages,
and had therefore an opportunity of gra-
tifying our sight a little; but our expec-
tations were by no means satisfied. The
city was doubtless immensely large, but
the buildings in general were low, and
had a mean appearance; the streets are
wide, but irregular, owing to different
houses and shops projecting out so far beyond others. The dwelling of the poor
and the opulent seemed strangely crowded
together, without any distinction: in many
places, a decent house, or tradesman's shop,
was joined to a mean mud-walled cottage;
but neither had windows, or any admit-
tance for light next the street: each had
an inclosure backwards, which in general
was planted with trees, which gave the city
a rural appearance. The streets were dusty,
and crowded with people of all ranks, as
on our first entrance; amongst whom were
many of the female sex, whose curiosity

exceeded that of the men. In the evening, we arrived at our old quarters at Teon- cheu; and the following day embarked once more on board some accommodation boats, and proceeded down the river. These vessels were much better provided than those we had in coming up, and con- siderably larger: provisions were also serv- ed out to us of a superior quality, and in greater variety and abundance; we had also the liberty of superintending the cook- ery on board, which we managed more in the English style. Fruit was also served out in great plenty; and, in short, we had a superfluity of necessaries and luxuries. Every town we passed, of any note, the people seemed anxious to give us some proof of respectful attention; the soldiers were drawn up under arms, and the guard turned out long before we appeared in sight. Landing places, with matting, and ornamented with variegated pieces of silk and calico, in case his Lordship chose to land, were erected at all the principal towns. In this manner we slowly proceeded, forgetting our disappointments in Pekin, and enjoying the beauties of the surrounding scene, and the bounties of indulgent Providence. On the 12th of October, we once more came in sight of the city of Tien Sing; where the mandarin, who had so respectfully treated us before, had provided an elegant entertainment in a temporary building, at the front of his own palace; in which the principal men of the city were posted, in their richest attire, and saluted us as we passed along with much civility; and the crowds of people gathered together along the banks of the river, for many miles, astonished us all. At a moderate computation, I will venture to affirm they exceeded two millions; and though the numbers were so immense, yet on the appearance of a mandarin, or soldier's whip, they gave way in a moment, without the smallest appearance of ill

nature; in fact, they durst not offer any
resistance, so strictly are they kept in subjection, and the slightest disobedience punished on the spot with such severity.

At Tien Sing we entered a different
river, and proceeded near a mile below the
city before we stopped. The old gentleman here gave us another proof of the
generosity and goodness of his heart; each
boat received a very handsome present of
provisions, fruit, and sweetmeats, in such
abundance, that we could not consume a
tenth part of it. The old man had gained
the entire affection of every one of us, by his
continued assiduity during our passage up
from Tien Sing, our stay in China, and
journey into Tartary; he had been our
constant attendant and provider, and never
ceased in any instance to convince his
Lordship, and the Embassy in general, of
his sincere wishes for its success. We
were equally sincere in our wishes, that

he might not leave us till we got to the
end of our journey, or inland voyage.
Under him, a great number of inferior
mandarins and officers attended us ; many
of whom also had been with us during
our stay in the country, and had become
very familiar. We had gained some knowledge of their language, at least so as to
ask for most things we wanted, which they
instantly procured ; we therefore wanted
for nothing to make us comfortable. We
thought ourselves happy, and did not re-
gret the length of time we were to spend
in our journey to the shipping, which we
were given to understand would take us
up a month or more. The weather was
cool, but pleasant; the harvest was all got
in, and the country on every side afforded
the most extensive and delightful prospect
imaginable. The roofs of the houses, erected on these accommodation boats, being
flat and pretty high, we could take a survey of the surrounding country; which

during the first thirty-three days was quite level, and nothing to oppose the prospect but towns and villages, which in many places were so thick and close together that we could scarcely discern the separation.

On the banks of this river, were many very large towns ; and on the morning of the 4th day from Tien Sing, we had a noble prospect of a large walled city; and at a considerable distance, after we had passed it, we could nearly see all round the walls, which in circumference might be about 3 leagues. The suburbs were mean and shabby mud-walled huts, which as you approach near the city hide it entirely from your sight. In the evening, just as darkness began to close around us, another city appeared on the banks of the river;—but a very imperfect sight of it. We observed a great number of soldiers encamped all along, who regularly turned

out under arms on our approach, and remained drawn up till after every boat had
passed them; and saluted his Lordship
with three guns, which is the most they
ever fire, except to the Emperor. Guns
they cannot properly be called, being nothing more than a piece of hollowed wood;
one end of which is stuck in the ground,
and filled with powder, is fired right into
the air; the report is equal to a small field
piece.

On the 12th, we entered the province
of Chan-tong, and had different mandarins and officers appointed to conduct us
forward to the next. Each boat had also
two soldiers, to see that none of the pas-
sengers absented themselves. It is astonishing what can induce them to be so jealous and fearful of strangers; for though
China is one of the finest and most desire-
able countries in the world, yet their manners and way of living bear such a contrast

to ours, that few would ever wish to stay
with them, that had any prospect of living,
though in the lowest style, at home. The
ignorance and superstition of the common
people here have no bounds; they have
scarcely an idea of there being any other
country than their own. In this province
in particular, I really believe, not one in
ten ever heard of any strangers passing
through it before this Embassy; every
thing was therefore a matter of wonder
and astonishment. If our boats passed any
town or village at midnight, thousands of
anxious gazers would crowd about them,
in hopes of gaining a sight of some of us;
and would follow the boats a considerable
time till they had satisfied their curiosity.

On the 22d of October, the course of
the river led us past a tower, built in a
very singular manner; it was something
like the porcelain tower at Nankin, of
which that in Kew gardens is built in imita-

tion; it was entirely of white brick, except between each story, which was ornamented with a kind of varnished tile : it had eight squares, about four yards each in circumference; and every square had a window, or space left for one; it was eight stories in height, beside the ground floor and cupola, and was about 240 high from the ground. Round about it, we observed a more than ordinary number of houses for their idol gods ; but generally in such bad repair, that we could easily see his godship through the ruins. The tower was built upon an extensive open plain, and about three miles from a small fortified city, of which we had but a faint prospect, though not more than gun-shot from the walls in many places ; it being surrounded (as their finest buildings generally are) by mean, dirty mud-walled huts. At this place we left the river, and entered a canal which was cut from it, but nearly equalled in width and depth the river itself.

On the 24th we passed two fortified
cities, where a great many soldiers were
stationed. Hereabout, and as we got further on, we saw many castles, or kind of
fortifications, but capable of no defence,
except against small arms, &c. The buildings in general, as we advanced more to
the southward, were better finished, and
not disgraced with so much dirt and mud
as many already taken notice of.

The 25th, the hilly country appeared on
our left, which we conjectured to be near
the sea coast ; and the country for two or
three days, as we advanced nearer to it, was
entirely overflowed with water; though
not an inch of it but seemed to be cultivated with great art. The people were
busy in getting the produce, which they
carried away in boats; and in other places,
the fishermen were collecting the finny
tribe. The methods they made use of were
various, according to the depth, or incon-

venience of weeds, which were great in many places; some with nets, others with baskets, contrived in a very artful manner, which afforded us much entertainment as we passed along. Wild fowl seemed also to be in great abundance; and we were told their method of procuring them was very singular, by concealing themselves among the weeds, and decoying the birds, so as to take them in their hands. The 26th and 27th, the canal took a winding course at the foot of some very pleasant hills, on every one of which towers and fortifications were erected, which afforded a charming prospect. There appeared to be a vast number of soldiers stationed in this part of the empire, particularly in the neighbourhood of the capital towns; but we thought it was so contrived by the mandarins, that we should pass most of those in the night time; but the military were always under arms, with lanterns posted in their front, so that we could easily

M

count them, and observe in what manner
they were armed.

On the 1st of November, pretty early in
the morning, we entered a spacious lake,
or large body of water, into which a number of fine rivers and canals emptied themselves. The prospect here was beautiful
beyond description; the country round it
exhibited such a variety of rural scenes,
that nothing I ever saw before could equal;
towns, villages, lawns, groves, hills, and
dales, so interspersed and mingled together, that nature seemed to have exhausted
all her store on this pleasing spot; the
lake too was covered with vessels, sailing
in a variety of directions, which added
much to the beauty of the prospect. About
the centre of the lake the current was asto-
nishingly rapid, and carried the vessels
away with such violence, that it was with
much difficulty the men could manage
them, or prevent their running foul of each

other; in fact, they seemed very diffident of their own abilities, or conceived themselves in great danger : they implored the aid of their gods to carry them through with safety, which haply they effected, though not without accident; one man fell overboard, and serjeant Stewart had also the misfortune to make a false step, but being an excellent swimmer, he supported himself till a boat was put out, and saved him. About noon we entered the Yellow river, or a canal, which carried us into it, on the 3d. Here we had an opportunity of observing one curious method of catching fish in the lakes, which abound in this part of the country ; two or three men in a small boat have about a dozen birds they call cormorants; they are as black as a crow, but considerably larger, with long yellow sharp-pointed beaks, and, on a signal being given by their masters, all dart suddenly into the water, and continue under till an oar or pole is thrown

alongside the boat, they then all rise upon
it, and discharge what fish they have procured into the boat, and wait for further
orders.

On the 5th of November we crossed
another beautiful lake, surrounded by
mountains, and full of high rocky islands,
on some of which pagodas and places of
worship were erected, which had a very
romantic appearance. At the foot of the
mountains there were several pretty villages, whose inhabitants were chiefly employed in building of junks, many of which,
and some monstrous large ones, we saw
on the stocks. Several of their war vessels
were lying here; but they were miserable
looking wrecks. On entering the river,
above the lake, we had to go under a
bridge, and found, as we advanced higher
up, many others; some had but one, and
others had three arches. They were all
built of stone, and of a surprising height,

but had nothing curious in the workman-
ship. The country hereabouts had quite a
different appearance from any part we had
hitherto seen. One day we were winding
round about the mountains, and the next, we
were surrounded by a low marshy country,
full of lakes and large collected pieces of
water; and never a day that we did not
go through one, and frequently two or
three, capital cities, all of which were better built the farther we went to the southward; trade also seemed to flourish more.
The rivers swarmed with vessels, all busi-
ly employed both night and day; in short,
every thing around us bespoke them a far
more ingenious and industrious people than
any we had seen since our arrival amongst
them. The mandarins, and all above the
common ranks, were clothed in silks. The
soldiers too, who were drawn up in their
uniforms, had a more splendid appearance;
with respect to their arms and accoutre-
ments, they differed but little from those

we had before seen. The cities and large
towns hereabout seemed very ancient; the
walls and houses were decaying very fast.
Its population exceeds even belief; it is
impossible for any one to conceive it, the
whole country is absolutely covered with
people, and every river is full of floating
houses; it is also wonderful to see what
numbers will nestle together, seemingly
without any inconvenience : where four
or five Englishmen would find themselves
straitened for room, ten or twelve Chinese will be as happy and as snug as possible. They live chiefly on vegetables,
which the country produces in great abundance : rice is also a favourite dish ; of this
grain they have two crops annually; they
were getting in the second as we came
through this province. A vast quantity of
silk, tallow, and camphor, is also got here;
for many days together we could see nothing but groves of those trees which produce the tallow, which is taken from a nut

or apple, exactly resembling, in colour and shape, that seen on potatoe stalks. The mulberry, the orange, and the camphor trees grow indiscriminately through the country, and have a most charming appearance. A vast variety of other fruits and useful articles of trade are found in this part of the country; but we were too confined to examine them with accuracy or attention, so as to give a true description. The Chinese in this part of the empire seemed, if possible, more anxious to see us than those nearer Pekin; and, from a request made by the mandarins, Colonel Benson issued an order that we should all appear on deck in passing through any of the towns. The country people, we were told, came upwards of an hundred miles merely to see us pass by, and seemed quite delighted when they were gratified with a momentary glimpse.

On the 15th of November we arrived at

Hon-geu, a very capital city, and strongly
fortified. It is not very common to meet
with any cannon in the empire, as it is an
article they are very awkward in using, and
very fearful of; but at the gates of this
place we saw seven or eight large field-
pieces, well mounted, and in good order;
and about six miles distant, we were received by several regiments of soldiers,
drawn up in the most regular and uniform
manner we had hitherto seen in our tra-
vels through the empire; some had bows
and arrows, others had matchlocks, and
about two regiments had swords and
shields only. In the centre of each batta-
lion were placed some pieces of artillery:
they continued saluting for some time, till
we had embarked on board some small
junks which lay ready for our reception.
Lord Macartney and the greatest part of
his attendants took the route for Canton.
Colonel Benson, Captain Mackintosh, Mr.
Alexander, Mr. Dinwiddie, and nine others

of inferior rank, took a different river for
Chusan Bay, where the Hindostan waited
for them. We received letters from on
board the Lion, to inform us she was
cruizing among the Ladrones, and in a
sickly condition. We parted at Hang-
cheu, and were all carried about eight
miles down to the beach in sedan chairs,
except the military, who marched in uniform order, at the request of the mandarins, to the place of embarkation, where
the whole country seemed covered with
people of all descriptions; and thousands
of soldiers, drawn up in such a manner,
that the Embassador and his train passed
through their ranks quite to the water's
edge, where temporary bridges were constructed upon waggons, and drawn by
buffaloes for near half a mile into the
water, it being so shallow that no vessels
could come nearer the land. The party
for Chusan crossed an arm of the sea, and
at sunset landed at a small village, about

30 miles from Nanking. Sedan chairs received us so suddenly, that we had scarce time to feel the ground before we were hoisted up, six feet above it, upon the shoulders of two lusty fellows, who trotted away with us for about half an hour; and then thrust us into dirty little boats, where we lay that night; and early next morning we were hauled along a canal, cut through a most delightful country for about 25 or 30 miles : it not being finished, or carried to the river to which it was intended, we were once more obliged to disembark at the city of Tin-chin-chee, from whence we were carried, as on the former day, in chairs, and thrust into them so indiscriminately, and with so little regard to persons, that some of the gentlemen were obliged to take up with very bad ones, open and ragged, and exposed on every side to chilly cold rain, which began to fall as we landed; while those of inferior rank were, in general, accommo-

dated with others as oppositely elegant
and comfortable. The next day, we were
no better provided, with respect to boats;
but for provisions, and luxuries of every
kind, we had in vast abundance, and superior of the sort to any hitherto received;
the country too was so delightful, that
every trifling inconvenience was readily
passed over. The mandarins also assured
us, that they would provide larger and
better junks as soon as the depth of water
would allow; but here the canals only ad-
mitted such small craft as those we occupied. The country was variegated and
hilly, so that we had to pass through several locks, very oddly constructed; they
were obliged to heave us up by means of a
windlass, and a rope passed round the
stern, till the head overbalances, and she
then launches down with great velocity on
the opposite side. The Chinese are very
active in the management of their boats,
or disagreeable accidents, and often dan-

gers, would happen in these inland navigations.

On the 14th, we reached the city of Hoong-pee, and as our mandarin attendants promised, were accommodated with very neat and comfortable vessels; but were so pestered with servants and soldiers, that we were heartily sick of our journey. Here we entered the hilly country, and on the 15th came in sight of the famous city of Nang-poo, situated on the side of a rugged mountain, as barren and uncouth as the hills in Derbyshire. What could induce them to erect so noble a city, in so rough a place, is astonishing, when you view it surrounded by plains as beautiful and fertile as any in China; but it is strong by nature and art, the ascent to it being almost perpendicular, except on that side next to the river, which is defended by innumerable forts, and the strongest I had seen in China. They treated us here with unusual respect, and honoured us with visits almost every hour in the day. The principal men seemed to have more curiosity than those of inferior order, and seemed delighted with our affability. They inquired about European customs, and compared them with their own with singular delight; and made their remarks on any thing about us that appeared unaccountable or odd. We would also ask frequently an explanation of any thing that appeared so to us; and in general they were more communicative than their countrymen had hitherto been, excepting some particulars which respected their religion; this seemed a mystery which they could not explain, nor could we form a judgment what they are, or in what belief. Their idols are numerous; every petty village, and almost every house of note, has its particular god for public or private worship; and no boat, however insignificant, is without, to which

they offer sacrifices and prayers, in time
of danger, and on particular days. The
custom of burying their dead, or rather of
disposing of them, disgusted us most of all:
a burial it cannot properly be termed, for
you might sometimes see thousands of
coffins wholly exposed, and the corpse in
a state of putrefaction; others were half
buried, or half covered with straw. Some
few have vaults, and a decent house
erected over, carvèd and ornamented with
curious images; and a few of their great
men, who have signalized themselves,
or have rendered any particular service
to their country, have a statue erected
to their memory at the public expence.
This particular custom is not common
all over the empire, nor indeed are any
customs; but each province varies and
differs from the neighbouring ones, as
much as though they had no connection
with each other: for instance, about Pekin and the province of Pet-chee-li, a

deep pit is made, and the corpse set upright in it, over which they raise a mound of earth near eight feet high, of an oval form, without any other token to signify whose dust it covers.

At Ning-poo the tea tree flourishes in greater perfection than any where else in China; it was in blossom as we passed, and every hill being covered with it, made the prospect truly pleasing. The orange, the camphor, and tallow-trees are also natives of this province, besides many other articles of trade and fruit, in such abundance that it is quite a drug. They carry on a great trade from this city to Batavia, the Philippine Islands, and other settlements in the Chinese seas, in their own vessels; and they supply the European ships, by way of Canton. The principal mandarins made each man a present of silks, tea, nankeen, tobacco, and other trifling articles, worth about three pounds, and

strove to render our stay as agreeable as
possible; but the weather proving bad, we
were detained too long amongst them to
be contented or happy. The wind was not
only contrary for us, but it blew a perfect
gale, and rained with such violence, that
it beat through the matting which covered
our junks, and almost drowned us; it also
continued without intermission for seven
or eight days. Being eager to get on board
the Hindostan, which lay at no greater
distance than ten leagues, made us very
fractious and impatient, which the mandarins took notice of, but did not appear
displeased.

On Thursday, December 4th, the wind
moderating, we got under weigh, and
sailed in a winding direction among pleasant hills, covered with the white blos-
soms of the tea shrub and others, which
refreshed us most agreeably with their
fragrance; and in addition to our pleasure,

about three o'clock, we came in sight of the Hindostan; who, on our nearer approach, saluted us with nine guns: she also received her commander under a second salute. The garrison and troops kept up an incessant fire for twó hours, and the next day they honoured our gentlemen with a grand review. The city of Chusan is built partly in a pleasant valley, and on the rise of a rugged hill; and defended by regular built forts on every rising ground about it. Its chief trade is with Canton, for tea and nankeens: they also manufacture a coarse calico, and a few handkerchiefs.

In two days after our arrival, having finished taking in the baggage, &c. belonging to the Embassador, we got up our anchor with a favourable breeze, and saluted the grand mandarins as we passed by the city. We were all in good spirits, and eager to reach Canton, where we

N

expected to meet numbers of our countrymen, and receive letters from our friends
at home. The wind blew fresh; and just
as we cleared the bay the ship struck violently upon a rock, causing great confusion on board, as we were fearful it was
all over with her, and perhaps with ourselves too; but happily she sheered off in
a few minutes, without receiving any apparent damage. As we opened the bay it
blew very hard, but the wind was in our
favour. On the 7th, we saw the island of
Formosa; and on the 8th, got among the
Ladrone islands. On the 9th, we entered
the Bay of Macao, and saw four large ships
riding at anchor off the city, but were at
too great a distance to distinguish what
they were. In the evening, we got a chop,
or passport, to enter the river. The two
forts at the entrance of the Bocca Tigris,
saluted us with three guns, and hoisted
the Emperor's colours as we passed. They
used formerly to receive and return sa-

lutes from all our Indiamen here; but
this practice had been disused since the
unhappy fate of the gunner at Canton,
mentioned in the former part of this Journal; it was an honour we did not expect,
to be received in so distinguished a manner, and therefore returned their salute
with two extra guns. Taking advantage
of the tide during the night to enter the
river, we passed the Lion without observing her, as she lay in Anson's Bay, just off
the Bocca Tigris. On the following day
we got up to the second bar, where we
found four of our Indiamen ready to sail
for Europe, viz. the Bombay Castle, Minerva, Chesterfield, and Brunswick; by
them we had the first intelligence of the
anarchy and confusion in France, and
of the war which was kindling throughout Europe. On the 3d of December,
we got up to Whampoo, the place where
all European ships lay to take in a
cargo: it is a very considerable village,

about sixteen miles below the city of Canton.

No ships are allowed to go higher up the river: the business of providing a cargo rests with the factors, who have most elegant houses in the city, and who live in splendour equal to many crowned heads. They reside here till the last, called the "book ship," sails for Europe, and then the Chinese oblige them to live at Macao till the first ship arrives the following season. The people at Whampoo having been so much used to Europeans, particularly our countrymen, that all of them have a little smattering of English, and some speak it fluently. As soon as the ships arrive, they are visited by tailors, shoemakers, washing girls, and boats, who supply them with a variety of things in English taste; and at Canton you may purchase almost any thing you want, which the merchants provide on purpose.

We found at Whampoo about twenty sail
of ships, from Holland, Sweden, Ostend,
and America; besides several British country vessels. The day after our arrival some
officers from the Lion came on board,
with letters from England; and on their
hearing of a war with France, she had
captured a French brig from the island of
Amsterdam, laden with furs; and chased
a large ship, which run on shore near
Macao. We had information, that several French privateers were cruizing in
and about the Straits of Sunda and Malacca, some mounting 30 guns, and full of
men; and a report was circulated that
they had captured the Princess Royal Indiaman. On the 6th of December, the
Warley Indiaman arrived; and on the
7th, the Royal Charlotte, Triton, and two
others arrived from Bengal. They informed us of the taking of Pondicherry;
and brought other interesting intelligence
from Asia, and from Europe. On the 11th,

a melancholy affair happened on shore:—it is usual for ships that arrive here to unrig entirely, and go through a thorough repair; and they have temporary storehouses erected, which they call the Banks Hall, for the armourers, carpenters, sail-makers, and other tradesmen, &c.; the steward of the Brunswick being ashore salting of provision for the voyage home, having some difference with a few seamen of that ship, was so rash and imprudent as to fire a pistol loaded with slugs amongst them, which killed one poor fellow on the spot, and wounded two others so dangerously, that their lives were despaired of; he was immediately secured in irons, to take his trial when the ship arrived in England.

On Friday the 20th of December, the four following ships arrived here from England; the Lord Thurlow, Earl of Abergavenny, Ceres, and Osterley; and three days after, the Glatton came in. By these ships, who sailed from the Thames in May, we had many letters; and all the news to that time. Our friends, who, as was beforementioned, parted from us at Hongeu, had to march through the city, which was so crowded with people, that they could scarcely get along; after which they embarked on a river, about eight miles from the city, on similar bridges to those already described; in a few moments after they were got on board, a number of buffaloes being yoked to the carriages, the bridges disappeared in a moment. About five the same evening, they set sail on the finest river they had ever seen, which bent its course along a fruitful valley, among hills covered with pagodas, and guard-houses for the soldiers, and neat cottages. On the 16th, the river divided itself into three or four parts; here a guard of soldiers, parading along the banks of the river, saluted his Lordship in a singular manner, by falling on their knees and

giving a loud huzza. This method of salu-
tation is practised by the Chinese to the
royal family and people of distinction,
and was never afterward omitted to his
Lordship during the journey to Canton.
The 18th, they arrived at a neat little village, where they were all drawn up; and
each man received a trifling present of
nankeen, fans, perfumery, &c. The river
on which they had now entered was so
shallow, that it required a number of men
to push the boats along, while other poor
shivering fellows were employed in rais-
ing the water from different falls, with
which the river abounded. There were a
number of mills situated upon it, employed
in grinding of rice. On the 20th, they disembarked, and were carried in chairs about
24 miles, passing through many villages
and cities, pleasantly situated. Orders were
issued that no man should, on any pretence whatever, leave his chair; but the
beauty of the surrounding scenery, and

pity to the poor objects who carried them, induced numbers to disobey : but this irregularity created much confusion ; some riding, others walking, made the line of march extend upwards of two miles, and rendered any orders that were given of no effect. Towards night, they entered an elegant little city, and were nobly accommodated with all they wanted during their stay, which was two days; and on the third, they once more embarked in small comfortable warm boats, and at night brought up alongside a large town, where a file of soldiers received them as before, with each of them an umbrella in his hand. Larger boats were provided, the river here being wide, and deep enough to admit them of any size. On each side houses were built on rafts of wood, and in which many families lived together, apparently in great harmony. These houses were continually moving up or down the river, seldom stopping more than a few days in a place. Some of these houses were very large, extending in length 200, and in breadth 100 yards; and had every convenience of the houses on shore, and even superior in many respects. Along the banks of this river were many fields of sugar-cane, of which the people seem remarkably fond; indeed it is their chief support. Around the villages and seats of the mandarins were large groves of evergreens and orange trees, laden with fruit in such a luxurious profusion, that no conception can be formed of the beauty of the prospect; in short, China is the finest country in the world with respect to its climate and production. I believe, there is nothing that is common in any other part of the world but is to be found here, and in equal perfection : it is peculiarly happy in the salubrity of the climate; and the inhabitants swarm all over the country like locusts : they are blessed with health, and live to a good old age; and but for the imperious manner in which they are governed, would certainly be the happiest people in the universe. But they are vain, licentious, uncivilized, and rude, when compared with the inhabitants of Europe. They fancy they exceed all other nations in antiquity, and in every other respect; and, though they could not help admiring the presents his Lordship brought from England, yet they affected to despise both the one and the other, as beneath their notice or imitation. In some things, they certainly excel all other people, such as china ware, porcelain, silks, &c. but had Great Britain the same materials to improve upon, the Chinese would sink into insignificance, and their trade with Europe dwindle into nothing.

They have a very ingenious method of watering the land, which we observed only in this province, and about Canton: the water is raised by wheels, according to the

height of the land, and is thrown a surprising distance through bamboo canes,
into a reservoir made to receive it, and
from that to another all over the country;
each wheel requires only two men to work
it, and throws up a great many tons in the
course of the day.

On the 9th of December we arrived at a
large walled town, where we disembarked,
and lay that night. In the morning each man
had a ticket given him, and was directed to
a large square, where a number of horses
ready saddled, waited for them; each man
pressed the best he could, and away he
scampered, helter-skelter, without waiting
for his Lordship, officer, or comrade: such
a motley group of horsemen perhaps never
appeared in any civilized country before.
The Chinese themselves were struck with
the novelty as we passed on, one, two, or
three, through the city, and for two miles
after we had got clear of it, and the coun-

try before us, away all drove like madmen;
and very few escaped without a fall, but
luckily all, without any material hurt.
Two horses were rode to death by the infantry; and many others disabled, before
half the day's journey was performed, which
was about 24 miles. The road was paved,
but narrow, and the country hilly; one
mountain we had to cross was so difficult
to mount, and so dangerous, owing to its
being almost perpendicular, that steps
were cut, to prevent horse or man from
slipping backward; one false step would
have plunged either headlong to the bottom, and he must inevitably have been
crushed to death; nor could the path be
made straight forward, but in a slanting
direction. From the summit of the hill we
had a most extensive prospect of the country before us, and the troop behind us, all
fearfully and cautiously endeavouring to
avoid the surrounding danger; which being accomplished, the same mad humour

and in this disorder and confusion we entered the city, where we had to stop that
night; and each as he entered was conducted down to the river side, and slept in
a palace belonging to the mandarin governor. The following morning, we once
more went into junks provided for us,
which were small and incommodious; and
on the 14th, we re-embarked in larger
ones, which brought us, on the 17th,
within about four miles of Canton. On the
18th, every man full dressed paraded on
shore; and were afterwards conducted to
some accommodation boats, the most completely elegant of any we had hitherto seen,
and dropped down the river, in a kind of
state, to the city, where a house was ready
provided for the reception of his Lordship;
or which might be more properly called a
palace; for of all the buildings seen, it
most deserved that title. It was originally
built by an English gentleman, partly in

the European and partly in the Chinese
taste, surrounded by gardens and pleasure-
grounds, so delightful and extensive, that
no just idea can be formed, or description
given worthy of it. The 25th (Christmas
day), most of the troops embarked on
board the Lion at Whampoo, his Lordship
reserving only a part of the royal artillery
to do duty over him.

The ships at the lower bar, viz. the
Bombay Castle, Minerva, Brunswick, and
Chesterfield, sailed for Europe the 30th of
December. January 2, 1794, arrived at
Whampoo the Lord Walsingham, Exeter,
and Hawke Indiamen. A seaman belonging to the Lion fell overboard this evening, and in spite of every exertion was
drowned.

On the 3d, the Henry Dundas arrived
from Madras; and on the 4th, a large
Spanish galleon, called the King Charles,

commanded by Don Ferdinando de Sylva, from Acapulco and Manilla, came in, and put herself under the protection of the British flag during her voyage home. The last Indiaman that arrived here from Bombay having come the eastern passage, had touched at Manilla, and informed the Spanish governor of their being at war with the French; and she being of immense value, did not care to run so great a risk as venturing through the Straits alone.

On the 8th, Lord Macartney and his suite came on board, and were received under a salute of 15 guns; the next day, the Lion unmoored, and on the 10th, weighed anchor, and dropped down through the Bocca Tigris. The 13th, we anchored in Macao Roads; and on the 15th, his Lordship and suite, attended by a detachment of his guard, landed at the city of Macao.

It is a Portugueze settlement on one of the Ladrone Islands; and it is a very considerable place, of large extent, and of great strength, having several forts on eminences round the city, which prevents its being approached either by sea or land. No large shipping can come within reach of it, the water being too shallow to admit them within the harbour, which is on the back of the town, and formed by another of the Ladrones. There are a great number of small shipping fitted out here; and since a trade has been opened between the north-west coast of America and China a great number of small craft touch here with the produce of that part of the world.

Macao is about sixty leagues from Whampoo, and about twenty from the entrance of the Tigris; it is inhabited principally by Chinese, who are under the government of a mandarin stationed here by the Emperor. It is computed that there

O

is about ten thousand of this nation and
one thousand Portugueze, besides factors
and merchants from almost every European nation. There are also a great number of Negro and Asiatic slaves. The city
is large, and contains some very elegant
buildings, both public and private. The
churches are numerous, and furnished, at
an enormous expence, with paintings and
images of bigotry and superstition. There
are several convents, and a college well
endowed, and some private schools for the
education of the lower class of people.

The city is well provided for defence
both by sea and land; the forts are all
built upon eminences, and command both
the harbour and the town; the former is
very secure for small ships, but the entrance is both difficult and dangerous, and
larger vessels are obliged to lay in the
roads, which are exposed to every wind
that blows. The Portugueze employ about

twenty vessels in the coasting trade, from one to four hundred tons burthen; they are fitted out here the latter end of February or beginning of March; and return about September, with the produce of A- sia and the north-west coast of America: These barter with the Chinese for teas, silks, china, anb various other commodi- ties for the Lisbon market. The ship- ping of Great Britain and other European nations, generally touch here as they go to Canton, and when they return to Europe. The supercargoes, and those who have the direction of the Company's affairs, reside here till the following season calls them to Canton. They are in general men of a liberal education, and spare no expence to live like gentlemen; in truth their houses, called factories, are palaces, and they are attended like princes.

The island is rocky and barren, and pro- duces scarcely any thing but vegetables;

but the neighbouring continent supplies it
liberally with every thing for the convenience and luxury of life, so that you may
procure whatever you want at a moderate
expence.

The other islands belong to the Emperor of China; they are all uninhabited,
but frequented by bands of piratical rovers,
from whose thievish dispositions the islands
received the name of Ladrones.

We arrived in the Lion off Macao on the
13th of January, 1794; his Lordship had
an elegant house ready for his reception,
and the gentlemen of his suite were lodged
in the British factory. His Lordship was
received on landing by his own guard, and
by the Governor of the island, who, with a
great number of Portugueze officers, and
all the principal people of Macao, came
down to the water side, and attended him
to the house of his Excellency the Gover-

nor. The most respectful attention was paid to the Embassy at this place it ever experienced; the forts, the churches, and even the convents, and places where no stranger was ever before suffered to enter, were thrown open; and everything curious or strange explained to them without any hesitation. They were astonished to find such a reception in a Roman Catholic country. The clergy themselves seemed anxious to outdo in civility the gentlemen in the civil or military line. The Swedish and Dutch factors also paid uncommon respect to the Embassy; in fact, every one who had any interest or influence at Macao exerted it to the utmost, to make our stay amongst them as comfortable as possible; nor were their good intentions thrown away, for not one, I believe, in the Embassy but regretted his departure, though for the purpose of returning to his native country. We continued at Macao till the 8th of March, when his Lordship and all

his suite embarked on board the Lion, in
the roads. A Portugueze ship, called the
Bon Jesus, joined us, along with the Spanish
galleon before mentioned from Whampoo.
The Indiamen were all to be ready for sea
by the 14th, and every necessary arrange-
ment made, so that nothing should delay
our sailing beyond that time. On the 11th
we stood over to Samcocks island, and
completed our stock of water.

On the 16th of March the following
Indiamen joined us from Canton, viz.
Hindostan, Royal Charlotte, Earl of Abergavenny, Hawke, Ceres, Osterly, Exeter,
Warley, Triton, Lord Walsingham, Henry
Dundas, Lord Thurlow, and Glatton; and
early on the morning of the 17th we got
under weigh, having also under our protection, the Spanish galleon, a Portugueze
frigate, the Jackall brig, and an American
ship. We had fine favourable breezes
across the Chinese seas, but were very

much detained by some of the Indiamen
who sailed remarkably dull. On the 28th
we saw the land bearing east-south-east,
distant about seven leagues; and the 29th
we passed by Pedro Blanca, a small black
rock standing by itself, and at the same
time had land on the starboard quarter,
bearing from us west-north-west, distant
ten leagues. About noon some of the
ships made a signal for seeing a strange
sail, and we immediately bore away after
her, and soon discovered her only to be a
small fishing boat. We had information
that several large French privateers were
cruizing in these latitudes, and were in
hopes of coming across some of them. All
hands were in high spirits, and anxious to
have a brush with their old and natural
enemy. I believe the Lion at this time
was in a better condition, either for a long
voyage or an action, than when she left
England. She had four hundred stout fellows on board, and not more than one or

two in the doctor's list   At noon this
day, we were in latitude 2° 24 north, and
105° 47' east longitude.

On the 31st of March we crossed the
Equator, and the 1st of April, saw the
island of Lingen, bearing south-west by
west, about seven leagues from us.   The
Asses' Ears, which are two sharp pointed
peaks on the centre of the high land, are
in 33' south latitude and 105° east longitude.   The small island of Pulo Taya was
easily distinguished, on our larboard quarter, bearing south-south-east, the wind
rather squally and unsteady.

On the 3d we anchored abreast of the
Seven Islands; Monopon Hill, at noon,
bearing south-south-east, distance ten
leagues; latitude by observation 1° 24'
south. Calms and light airs of wind these
several days past, with much thunder,
lightning, and heavy rain.

On the 4th we saw the island of Sumatra, and entered the Straits of Banca. On
the 6th, light airs of wind and calms. We
had a strong current against us, so that
we were obliged frequently to come to
an anchor. The weather was extremely
hot, which occasioned us to repine much
that we had not a stronger breeze, to
hasten our passage through the Straits,
and into a cooler latitude. By observation
this day, 1° 53′ south. At 4 A. M. saw a
ship at anchor under the land, on the
Banca side; at 9 she fired two guns, and
hoisted the Hon. the East India Company's colours, which we mistook for
American, from their similarity to each
other. The Jackall spoke her, and informed us, it was the Nancy grab, from Bombay. She had been chased near the Straits
of Sunda, by four French privateers; and
it was the general opinion, that they were
lurking about to pick up some of our
homeward bound Indiamen; and we were

in hopes of catching some of them, as they probably had not any intimation of our strength, and taking us for a fleet of lumbered India ships, might be daring enough to attempt making a capture: we much wished to find them in such a disposition.

On Monday the 7th, we saw several strange ships in the south-east quarter, and made a signal for the Exeter and Hindostan to chase They had a very suspicious appearance; one or two was under sail, and others getting under weigh. When they first saw us, they bore down before the wind, and a short time afterwards, stood away to windward, with all the sail they could carry. One of them made a signal, but not being answered, she stood across towards the island of Nanka. Our ships presently came near enough to distinguish a brig, and about a dozen large proas full of men; the former had eighteen carriage guns, and the others from

two to six each. The Hindostan fired
a shot to bring them too; but they not
minding it, both ships fired several guns
amongst them; and finding they could
not escape they anchored, and suffered
our boats to overhaul them. The brig was
Dutch built, and probably had been captured by the Malays, being manned entirely by those savages; and, no doubt,
they were cruizing about here with no
good intent. But suspicion only was not
sufficient to authorize our making a capture of them; they were therefore left towards evening, and the ships that had
overhauled them returned to their respective stations in the fleet.

On the 8th, we anchored off Hog Island;
calms, and light airs of wind. The next
day we cleared the Straits, and stood away
south-south-east; this and the two days
following, we had some heavy squalls of
wind; several of the Indiamen received

some trifling damage, which occasioned considerable delay to the rest of the fleet. On the morning of the 11th, it was very thick and hazy, till about 9 o'clock, when it cleared up, and we discovered two strange ships on our lee quarter; we immediately bore down upon them, and observed them to hoist the English union at the mizen peak, which immediately hauling down, they shewed a blue ensign, and afterwards a Dutch jack at the mizen-top-gallant-mast head: after this they hauled upon a wind, and crowded all the sail they could. The Exeter, being pretty near the stern-most ship, fired a gun to bring her too, the other hoisted a private signal to alter her course. By this time we had cleared our ship, run out the lower deckers, and were ready for action, not doubting but they were some of the French cruizers. I never saw such alacrity, such spirit, and such anxiety as appeared throughout the Lion during the chase. The moment the drum beat to quarters every one obeyed the summons as cheerfully as though they had been ordered to splice the main brace. In less than half an hour, every gun was loaded, and the ship as clear as if she was just out of dock. The men threw away their own lumber, and the officers assisted to demolish their cabins; so that, fore and aft, nothing was seen but guns, ammunition, lighted matches, and various instruments for the destruction of mankind. Every inch of canvas was spread before a favourable breeze, and we could perceive that we gained fast upon them; when about noon the headmost ship once more hoisted the British flag, lowered her top-gallant sails, and saluted with fifteen guns; this done, they bore down towards us. The Lion unshotted some of her upper-deck guns, and returned the salute. The Exeter was ordered to speak her, and we soon found them to be two ships fitted out from Bengal, to clear these seas of the French pri-

vateers. Their being friends and countrymen did not give us half the satisfaction
we should have received, to have found
them our old and natural enemies, whom
we wished to have a brush with. Each
seaman and soldier left his quarters in
sullen disappointment. The can of grog,
which soon followed, revived their spi
rits, and many a hearty loyal toast rung
throughout the ship. Captain Mitchell,
Commodore of these, and some other English ships at Batavia, came on board, and
gave us the following intelligence : that the
Governor General of Bengal, hearing of the
capture of the Princess Royal Indiaman,
in the Straits of Sunda, and of the increasing strength of the French privateers in
these seas, had ordered the Britannia,
Captain Cumming; Nonsuch, Captain
Hudson; Houghton, Captain Cheap; and
the William Pitt, Captain Mitchell, to be
fitted out to go in search of them. They
sailed from Bengal in December, had cap-

tured two French ships, one of 32, the
other of 24 guns, in the Bay of Bengal.
By them they understood the enemy was
lurking about near the Straits of Malacca,
and that they had fitted out the Princess
Royal with 52 guns and 550 men. Beside
this ship they had two others, one of 50
guns, and 500 men, named the Bourdeaux;
the other of 44 guns, and 400 men, called
the Sybile; the armed brig Prudente, of 36
guns, and 300 men, and a sloop of war.
The English ships carried from 36 to 44
guns, and were in other respects well provided to give them a warm reception. The
Princess Royal not having destroyed her
signals, they of course fell into the hands
of the enemy, and made use of them to de-
coy Captain Mitchell, who took them for
friends, till he received a broadside; this
happened off Pulo Babey, near Batavia;
they fought a long time, but the French
were beat off. Prior to this action they had
taken the Resolution and the Revenge, two

of the ships above mentioned. The Pigot Indiaman had a gallant action with both of these privateers, which lasted almost an hour; she however beat them off, and got into Bencoolen roads. The other French squadron succeeded better, they cut her out of the roads, and got clear away. Captain Mitchell also informed us, that two frigates, one under royal, the other under national colours, came into port near Batavia. East of Java head they fought an obstinate battle; but the democrats were beat, and the prisoners sent ashore amongst the Malays, who in all probability did not treat them much better than their countrymen, and the royalists returned after the action to Old France.

The William Pitt had the misfortune to run upon a rock going into Batavia, and was obliged to be hove down to Enroost. The Houghton lay there at present as a guard-ship to protect the Dutch, who were busied in fitting out some vessels to join our squadron. This was the principal intelligence we received from these two ships: they at first mistook us for the enemy, it being so hazy they could not see above three or four of our ships. By an American ship, which they spoke in the Straits, they learnt that we were ready for sea, and as the fog cleared away, by our number, they were not long in doubt who we were. They returned with us to North Island, where we anchored early on Sunday morning, the 13th instant. The Nonsuch and Britannia captured two American ships, which they sent into Batavia: though under American colours, they were French bottoms, and had French property on board. We lay in our old station only till the following morning, and then stood over towards Java. At noon we anchored near Angeree Point, with the Spanish galleon and five of our Indiamen. On hoisting our colours, we were presently visited by a

P

Dutch serjeant (who had long been resident there), with plenty of turtle, goats,
fowls, and fruit, and informed us, that the
brig we had overhauled in the Straits of
Banca, was taken by some Malay proas,
and the crew, consisting of about thirty
Dutchmen, were all inhumanly murdered.
Sir Erasmus Gower had expressed some
dissatisfaction that she was not brought
along with us, till his suspicions were
cleared up; and he could not forbear in-
veighing in bitter terms against the officers
of the Indiamen who boarded her, for suffering her to escape them so easily; and
all hands were vexed that these savages,
whose inhumanity we had experienced,
should not meet with the punishment they
so justly merited, both from ourselves and
the Dutch; and in all probability so good
an opportunity might not offer again.

The Dutch serjeant also told us, that the
King of Bantam had performed the promise

made to his Lordship, prior to our departure from hence to China last year, and had revenged the death of poor Lightring, the draughtsman, who was murdered at the watering place, near North Island: he had found the persons who had committed the horrid deed, and put them all to death in a cruel manner. The buoy belonging to an English ship was left here; some French cruizers had forced her to slip her cable, and get out. We could not understand the names of either of the vessels; but the action happened only two days before our arrival; and in all probability the French were successful. The engagement between the Princess Royal and three privateers, was in sight of the Dutch, at Angeree Point, and was obstinately maintained for an hour; but superior numbers at length prevailed, and she was obliged to strike the flag she had so gallantly strove to defend.

On the 15th, the ships began to come over from North Island, and all arrived by the following evening, with the Nonsuch and Britannia.

The 17th, we completed our sea stock of wood and water, and were all ready for sea. Before we quitted Angeree Point, we had several proofs of the thievish disposition of the Malays; there was scarcely a boat went ashore from our ship, or the Indiamen, but they made some attempt upon; several of them were desperately wounded with the axes of the wooding parties, who spared none that appeared suspicious, but drove them back into the woods to their lurking places, bruised and wounded in a shocking manner: but nothing could prevent these savages from attacking our people whenever they appeared to have an advantage. We had large parties washing on shore, near the watering place and they

were artful enough to convey several shirts
and other articles away unperceived. We
detected one carrying off a shirt, and pursued him a considerable way; but he got
clear by concealing himself amongst some
cocoa trees; and when they found that we
were aware of them, they were quite impudent, and made several daring attempts
upon our people. One fellow had the resolution to attempt carrying off some waist-
coats, which one of my comrades was
hanging upon some poles; and came steal-
ing behind him with his dagger drawn,
and his hand uplifted, to plunge it into his
heart: some bushes prevented him seeing
his danger till he got within five or six
paces; when turning suddenly about, and
perceiving the Malay irresolute, whether
to advance or retreat, he hallooed to his
comrades, who coming up immediately to
his assistance, caused the fellow to make
off. The soldier, whose name was Stephen,

had no weapon of defence but a stone, which he threw after the rascal with great force, and was near hitting him upon the head, which if it had, would have prevented his running much farther.

They seemed very inveterate against the crew of the Spanish ship; they attacked them on shore repeatedly, and took several articles from them by force. It is astonishing that seven or eight Dutchmen, which are all the Europeans settled at Angeree Point, can keep the Malays in such awe and subjection as they do; but the neighbourhood of Batavia and Bantam may be the principal reason : the Dutch are very powerful on the Island of Java, and they are also favoured by the King of Bantam, who keeps the petty princes in subjection; in fact he himself is only a prisoner to the Dutch, and made answerable for the misdemeanours of his subjects.

April 17th, two Dutch brigs came round from Batavia; they were cruizing to protect the country trading vessels against the Malays; but brought no particular news.

At daybreak on the 18th, the Lion made a signal to unmoor, and about 2 o'clock A. M. all the fleet were under sail, with a favourable breeze from the south-east. We parted from our old companion the Jackall in the Straits, and she joined the squadron under Captain Mitchell, who purposed cruizing some time longer near Batavia, in expectation that the French might again return to that quarter. Having now a long voyage before us, and to prevent any of the ships separating themselves from the fleet, Captain Sir Erasmus Gower issued a number of additional signals, to be used in the night, and in thick foggy weather; and he particularly cautioned the different commanders to keep

in close order of sailing. Some of the Indiamen were intolerable dull, heavy sai-
lers; the Portuguese in particular detained
the whole fleet; five or six knots an hour
were the most we could get out of her,
in a breeze that would have carried us
nine or ten. The 19th we were entirely
out of sight of land; the wind steady, and
the weather remarkably pleasant; we soon
caught the regular trades, which, within
the tropics, blow invariably from the eastward: our course west-south-west.

The 25th, we had been out seven days,
and in that time had made upwards of
1800 miles on our course, being, by observation, in latitude 11° 39′ south, and
93° 50′ east longitude; distant from the
Cape of Good Hope 1456 leagues. The
29th, we lost sight of the Lady Washington.

On the 30th, we were in latitude 17° 36′

south, 76° 55′ east longitude: Cape of Good
Hope distant 1104 leagues.

May 1st, lat. 18° 32′ S. 74° 12′ east long.
the Cape, half west, distant 1043 leagues.
The American rejoined the fleet, which
were all in tolerable close order of sailing.
Strong breezes, and squally, with frequent
heavy rains. The prospect of making a
speedy passage across the Southern Ocean
kept all hands in good spirits, though they
were but in a sickly condition. Since leaving the Straits of Sunda, the greatest care
was taken to prevent the disorder being universal, by washing and smoking between
decks as often as the weather would permit. Made signals for the Hindostan,
Glatton, and Abergavenny to give their
longitude, which answered to our own
within a few miles.

May 2d, altered our course one point
more westerly, and stood west by south:

the Mauritius bore west, about 800 miles
distant.

The 3d, squally weather, and much
rain. All the ships in pretty close order
of sailing except the American, who was
so far astern, that we could only just discern her from the mast head. Required,
by signal, the state and condition of some
of the Indiamen, who were in general in
a sickly way; but in other respects, tolerably well provided for the long voyage
before us.

On the 4th, the wind died away entirely;
and we were becalmed until the evening,
when we got a gentle easterly breeze; latitude 20° 13′ south, 67° 27′ east longitude;
the Mauritius west, distant 573 miles.

May 5th, in latitude 21° 26′ south, 65°
26′ east; 904 leagues distant from the
Cape of Good Hope. Squalls, and heavy

gales of wind from the southward. On the 6th, moderate breezes, and steady weather; latitude 22° 25′ south, 62° 44′ east; distant from the Cape 842 leagues.

Fine gentle breezes, and clear weather on the 7th. At daybreak, the Ceres Indiaman made a signal for a strange sail to windward, then standing the same course as ourselves; the Lord Thurlow was directed to chase; she came up about noon, and found her to be an American brig, called the Hancock, from Canton to New York; out two months.

May 8th, made a signal for the longitude of the following ships:

Abergavenny	-	55° 31′ east.
Exeter	-	56 9
Hindostan	-	56 10
Henry Dundas		56 32

Our own latitude, by observation, 24° 28′ south, 56° 10′ east longitude. Fine moderate winds from the eastward, and clear pleasant weather: course west by south.

May 9th, altered our course to west. Calms and moderate breezes from the southward. The ships all busy in bending new canvas, and getting the rigging, &c. prepared for a brush in doubling the Cape, which we did not expect to pass without meeting a hard gale of wind. By this day's reckoning, we were distant from it 578 leagues.

	latitude.	east long.
May 10th, we were in	26° 37′ south	51° 22′
11th, —	27° 13′ —	50° 37′
14th, —	28° 51′ —	40° 44′

leagues.
Distant from Cape 426, course due west.
May 15th, — 373, nearly calm.
16th, — 358, light east^{ly} winds.

leagues.

May 17th, from Cape 338, light easterly
winds.

18th, 302, ditto.

Latitude 32° 29′ south, 35° 42′ east longitude.

May 19th, a violent gale of wind came on from the westward, which blew with violence until the evening of the 20th, when it abated considerably, and veered a little more round to the southward, so that we could lay our course, which was west by south. The Glatton had the misfortune in a squall to lose her mizen-top-mast. The lightning struck her at the head of the mast, and proceeding downwards, shivered it to pieces: it forced its way through the decks into the round-house, where much damage was done; but providentially no lives were lost. From the round-house it got into the steerage, forced several ports open; and for some time they

were under strong apprehensions that the
ship had taken fire, for the people between decks could not see each other for
the smoke it occasioned. The violent claps
of thunder also rendered the scene truly
alarming. A ball of fire passed between
our fore and main-mast, and fell to leeward, without doing us the least damage;
though the seamen were crowded together
pretty close on the deck, and on the top-
sail yards. One man only felt the shock
of it, which laid him on his back, and left
him, for some minutes, deaf and speechless.

On perceiving the disabled situation of
the Glatton, we immediately stood towards
her, and hoisted out the yawl, in which we
sent her two carpenters to assist in repairing her damage : but she did not get her
mast and rigging up again till the 23d. The
weather continued pretty moderate all that
time, until towards evening a heavy gale
once more sprung up from the north-west,

which for about twenty-four hours blew with dreadful violence. The Royal Charlotte, the Portuguese frigate, and the Lady Washington, American ship, parted from the fleet the same night; and the following day the Lord Walsingham was also missing. Our old companion the Hindostan, had the misfortune during the gale to spring her fore-mast, and disable her main-top-mast, in such a manner that she was obliged to drop astern to repair her damage. Most of the fleet having suffered more or less, we continued under an easy sail till the 27th, to give them an opportunity to repair, &c. The wind was moderate and steady from the northward, with fine clear weather. On the 26th, latitude, by observation, 37° 26′ south, 24° 46′ east longitude: distant from the Cape of Good Hope, 116 leagues.

The longitude of the under mentioned vessels were:

Earl of Abergavenny, 24° 45′ east longitude
Exeter, - - - 24° 30′ ditto
Hindostan, - - 24° 22′ ditto
Osterly, - - - 24° 47′ ditto

The state and condition of the different ships were required: they had from four to ten men in the sick report, and from forty to seventy days water left. The crew of the Lion were in a very sickly condition, having near seventy men on the doctor's list, and many of them in a dangerous way. Since leaving Angeree Point, we had lost six seamen and a boatswain's mate; all of them carried off by the flux.

The Portuguese frigate rejoined the fleet on the 28th; and the same evening another violent gale of wind came on from the north-west, which continued about twelve hours, and separated six more of the ships from us. The 29th, the wind rather moderated, but continued variable till the evening of the 30th, when it came on suddenly in a squall, and blew with much greater violence than either of the preceding gales; the sea was excessive high, and broke over us in a tremendous manner, sweeping every thing away before it; for two days it continued thus violent, and entirely separated the fleet; only the Lord Thurlow remained in company with us, and we had great reason to be alarmed for the safety of the Hindostan, who had not sufficient time to have repaired the damage she had sustained in the late gale. The weather was so thick and hazy, that we could form no conjecture whether the ships in general were to windward or leeward of us; but we had the pleasure to see several of them standing towards us, early in the morning of the 1st of June. The Spaniard was the first we distinguished, and immediately answered the signal, by hoisting his colours at the main-top-gallant-mast head, and be-

Q

fore night twelve others rejoined us, and bore down into their respective stations. The Hindostan was still missing, nor could any of the other ships give any intelligence of her, or the Glatton. The Earl of Abergavenny had carried away her mainyard, and was otherwise much damaged; nor was it in our power to render her any assistance, our best carpenters being still on board of the Glatton, and those we had left were so much employed in repairing our own damages, as we had shipped a great quantity, and were obliged to keep pumping her every hour. Our rigging had suffered considerably as well as the sails; the main, mizen, and foretop-mast stay-sails; the fore and maintop-sail were torn to rags, the ship rolled so excessively, that we were at last obliged to lay her too under a balanced mizen; and even after the gale abated, the sea was so very high that we were in danger of rolling our masts overboard, before we could set sufficient sail to keep her steady.

June the 1st, we were, by observation, to the southward of the Cape of Good Hope about four degrees, and one degree to the eastward of it, being in 38° 11′ south, and 19° 37′ east.

June 2d, moderate breezes, but contrary. We stood away to the northward in latitude 38° 6′ south, 18° 22′ east longitude.

June 3d, light and variable airs 37° 0′, 17° 35′. Ten ships in sight. The Glatton, Hindostan, Royal Charlotte, Warley, Hawke, with the Portugueze and American still missing. This day the Hindostan, the Portugueze, and American ships rejoined us. The Lord Thurlow was ordered to go as far on our weather bow as she could distinguish signals, and look out for those ships still missing. Steady breezes from the south-west. The fleet was ordered to keep a N by W course.

June 4th, in latitude 36° 46′ south, longitude 16° 39′ east. St. Helena N 43 W distance 572 leagues.

June 5th, in latitude 35° 17′ south, longitude 15° 17′ east. The Lord Thurlow made signal for a strange sail ahead, which we came up with and spoke about two o'clock; she was called the Margaret of Boston, from the N W coast of America, and bound for China. On the 25th, she was spoke by the Fort William, Marquis of Lansdown, and another Indiaman from Bengal, in 57° c′ east longitude, and in the latitude of the Cape; by them she was informed that the French privateers had done considerable damage in the Bay of Bengal, and in its neighbourhood; she had no other information worth attending to. In the evening we made sail to rejoin the fleet to leeward, advising the Lord Thurlow to keep a look out to windward. The Hawke rejoined the fleet on 6th. This, and some following days we had a fine fresh breeze, which carried us into the regular trades within the Tropic.

On the 7th, we found ourselves in latitude 31° 34′ south, longitude 12° 42′ east; the 8th, in 29° 36′ south, 9° 57′ east. We saw a great number of grampusses in these latitudes, and vast flights of birds of a spotted colour, which they call Cape hens. The Exeter was ordered on our weather, the Lord Thurlow on our lee, bow, and the Henry Dundas ahead to look out for our missing, or for strange ships, but to keep within sight of us, that we might distinguish each other's signals.

The 10th, 11th, and 12th, we had light airs of wind and calms. By observation

on the 12th, we were in latitude 24° 49′
south, 4° 27′ east longitude; distant from
St. Helena 253 leagues.

On the 13th, we crossed the Tropic line,
and had a fine smart east breeze. On Sunday the 15th of June, we were in latitude
20° 20′ south, and in the longitude of London by the best calculation. Made signal
for the fleet to north-west by west, in expectation of making St. Helena in two or
three days. The sick on board began
to increase exceedingly, having near 100
men on the doctor's list, and most of them
very bad. At sunrise on the 18th, the
Exeter and Abergavenny being ahead,
made a signal for seeing land, and several
strange sails. We hoisted several signals,
which they not answering, the ships were
cleared for action, and the fleet directed to
bear down into their respective stations:
we soon discovered two of the strange
ships to be men of war; one appeared to

be a ship of the line, and the other a frigate : they hoisted British colours, and
bore down towards us, and proved to be
the Sampson of 64, and the Argo of 44
guns, sent out to convoy the East India
fleet from St. Helena; they sailed from
England the 22d of March, and this was
the first of their making land. The other
ships were from Bengal. At noon, St. Helena bore west by north, distant two leagues.
The land appeared high, rocky, and barren. About 2 P. M. we anchored opposite
the town, and were saluted from the fort
on Ladder Hill with 15 guns, which we
returned with an equal number. The island
of St. Helena is in 16° south latitude, and
6° west longitude; it is about twenty-one
miles in circumference, mostly high and
barren land; it produces no grain whatever, and has not pasturage sufficient to
support cattle for the consumption of the
inhabitants. In the valleys they raise vegetables and fruit; for every other article

they depend on England. The East India
Company send annually two store-ships
with beef, flour, &c.; and the ships from
China, and the East Indies, who all touch
here on their homeward bound passage,
generally leave something, so that there is
seldom a deficiency of either necessaries
or luxuries at St. Helena. It belongs to
the East India Company, who have fortified it very strongly; and they have generally from 500 to 1000 troops in garrison,
so that it would be a difficult matter to de-
prive them of it : it is the only place where
their shipping are allowed to stop from
India for a supply of water. There are
about 200 English families settled upon
it, mostly officers and servants in the Company's service.

We found, in the Roads, an English
whaler, and several ships from Bombay,
besides the Warley and the Glatton, who
parted from us in the gale of wind off the

Cape of Good Hope. The Royal Charlotte
came in the day after us. The Duke of
Buccleugh store-ship arrived from England
on the 20th; the Hancock, American brig,
from China, on the 26th; and the Belvidere and Fitzwilliam Indiamen, from Bombay, on the 27th. On the 30th of June, the
fleet having completed their stock of water,
a signal was made to unmoor, and early
in the morning of July 1st, all the ships
weighed anchor ; the signal was made to
form the order of sailing, which was as
follows :

H. M. S. Sampson,
H. M. S. Lion,

Abergavenny,	Lord Thurlow,	Glatton,
Hindostan,	King Charles,	Exeter,
Henry Dundas,	Bon Jesus,	Warley,
Ceres,	Royal Charlotte,	Osterly,
Hawke,	Fort William,	Lord Walsingham,
Triton,	M. of Lansdown,	General Coote,
Belvidere,		Fitzwilliam,

H. M. S. Argo.

Orders given out to Commanders of Ships by Sir Erasmus Gower.

" Suppose I make the signal that I wish you to sound, you will make the signal, that you have got ground or otherwise; that being answered, you will proceed to explain the depth of water, by shewing the number expressing the depth : the same to be done by the latitude, longitude, and variation; after having shewn the signal of either of the above, shew first the number expressing the degrees, and then the minutes.

" When your signal is made to look out to chase, or for any other occasion, the quarter of the compass you are to proceed in will be shewn, after having acknowledged understanding the signal.

" When the signal is made for a boat, or the ships have communication with each other, the days works are always to be exchanged.

" All signals will be made without guns, when it can be done with the same effect; nor will signals be confined to the top-gallant-mast head, or yard-arms, but when necessary, hoisted upon the lower-mast heads, studding-sail booms, mizen peak, &c.

" In all questions that are asked, or signals made, the answering flag is to be displayed; and must never be hastily shewn, it being highly necessary the signal made should first be perfectly comprehended.

" The duplicate flag hoisted alone, being the signal that a man has fallen overboard, is always to be kept bent, in a part of the

ship where there are people always ready
to hoist it.

" As you are in possession of the flags that
constitute these signals, you will have it in
your power to ask or give all the information you can wish. The safety and comfort
of the ships depending in a great degree
upon their keeping company together;
whilst the consequence that will even-
tually take place, even from a partial separation, is so obvious, and speaks so forcibly
for itself, that it leaves little for me to say
upon the subject.

" The sail that is to be carried during the
night will always be shewn before dark :
the same precaution in the day, on the appearance of fogs, or thick weather, from
which there will be no alteration in the
night, or when the weather is bad in the
day, except from violence of winds, or in-
cidents unforeseen.

" It is highly necessary, in order to avoid
separation as much as possible, that the
captain and officers be very attentive to ac-
quire a perfect knowledge of the compara-
tive rate of sailing between their own, and
the commanding officer's ship, so as whatever sail he may be, when there shall be
a change of weather, so as to obscure the
seeing of each other, they may know what
proportion of sail to carry, to go at an
equal rate with him.

" In moderate weather, or when the ships
are perfectly under command, the distance
from each other must not exceed one cable's length; and they must steer immediately in each other's wake, the lines to be
separated about two cables' length.

" In bad weather, or when inclinable to
calms, the distance must be extended; and
I think there is more danger to be apprehended, in getting on board each other, in

calms than in storms; and it is a very mistaken notion, and must not be put in practice, for ships to quit their stations in the night, under pretence of self-preservation; for if each ship acts for itself, every danger is to be apprehended.

" When in chase, you are to give notice as early as possible of your opinion of the vessel, or vessels, and that opinion you are to change as often as you find it necessary.

" When upon different tacks, the ship on the starboard one is to keep the wind, and the one on the larboard constantly to give way.

" In wearing, the leewardmost ship to wear first; and in tacking, the weathermost is the first to change her situation; when the wind is not fair, the ships will notwithstanding steer a little from it; that is, al-

ways by the compass, probably about half
a point from the wind, so as to preserve
their stations as near as possible; this
will have other advantages, that of pre-
serving the reckonings, and keeping company.

" When I wish the ship you command to
go ahead in the night, to carry a light, and
be on the look out, I will make the signal
for such service before sunset, at the same
time placing that sail upon the Lion I
mean to carry for the night; and we are to
keep half a mile asunder: and should you,
while on that service, have even your suspicions of danger, I would have you make
the signal by which the fleet may most
readily avoid it, and stand from it, or bring
too, which ever may be most proper at the
time; for upon this occasion, risk is not
to be placed in competition with an hour
or two's time.

" In sailing by the wind, if I am put by a sudden shift of it on the other tack, and should I have you change after me on that tack, I will make the proper signal for tacking.

" When in line of battle, and I should choose to quit that situation, I shall make the signal for the ships to continue the same course, though I act otherwise. The vacancy that I leave, must then be filled up by the rear closing. The same is to be observed respecting any vacancies that may be made by any of the ships having quitted the line, by signal or otherwise. When any signal respects the men of war only, a white pendant with a blue fly will be shewn at the same time : and if any particular ship, or ships, should be wanted to assist in performing the duty that the men of war are employed upon, their signals will be made.

"If I should at any time think it necessary
to form the line of battle, without attending to the prescribed order, the signal for
that purpose will be made when the ships
are to form ahead or astern of the Lion, in
the most convenient station that can be effected, with the least loss of time; but if
there should be time to form the regular
line, it will always be done upon the lee division; the weather division going from
the wind under a press of sail, will form the
van of the fleet; the centre division will
likewise bear up a little, under a more moderate sail, until they get ahead of the
lee division, which will then become the
rear, and each ship will haul her wind
when she brings the lee division in her
wake, or steer such course as may be directed by the commanding officer.

" In case of separating and meeting
again in the day time, the ship is to shew
her distinguishing pendant at its proper

mast-head, which will be answered by the
answering jack; but if the separated ship
should join us in the night, the hailing and
answering, will be the questions and an-
swers pointed out by the Admiralty.

" When I am going to make a signal in
the night, a rocket will occasionally be
fired, as a preparation; and in dark or
cloudy weather, one or more rockets will
be fired, to denote the situation of the commanding officer. Being in distress, fire
one or more guns, and the nearest ship
is hereby required to give every assistance."

A great many other orders and regulations were adopted for the conduct and
general. safety of this valuable fleet, in
case of falling in with any of the enemy's
cruizers or fleets on the voyage home, as
there was sufficient reason to apprehend
they would, if possible, endeavour to make

a capture of some of us. The Lion was put in as good a state, as it was possible, to make a gallant opposition; and though she was rather under-manned, yet what seamen she had were good, and in high spirits, and there was no doubt but if called to action, they would behave as nobly as could be expected by their most sanguine well-wishers. The Sampson and Argo had each their full complement of men, and were fitted out with every advantage, for the purpose of defending the ships from India. The former was ordered to keep a look out right ahead, and the latter on our larboard beam, as far distant as signals could be distinguished, and to close in with the fleet each night, while the Lion kept just ahead of the Indiamen, so as to direct the movements of the whole. The Washington, American ship, and the Lucas of London, a small ship from the southern whale fishery, left St. Helena in company with us. The American

parted company on the 3d of July, and
stood away to the westward for Philadel-
phia, after saluting the Lion with fifteen
guns, which she returned with nine. For
some days we stood N N W between the
Coast of Guinea and the Island of Ascen-
sion, and St. Thomas's. We afterwards
stood away N W, and crossed the Equinoctial line on the 12th, in the longitude of 20°
west, with fine steady breezes from the S E.
On the 14th, we bore away due north, and
on the 15th a signal was made to steer N
by E. We had most delightful weather
near the Line, and were amused by shoals
of bonattas and dolphins chasing the poor
flying fish. From this to the 22d we had
variable weather, with squalls of heavy rain
and calms; the wind blew chiefly from
the northward and westward. Early on
the morning of the 21st of July, one of the
Indiamen made a signal for seeing strange
sails, and the Sampson fired a gun to signify that a fleet was discovered. As it

cleared up we could distinguish eleven
sail, some of which appeared very large.
We immediately hoisted the ensign at the
main, and union at the fore-top-gallant
mast-head, being the private signal for the
day, as appointed by the Lords of the Admiralty. They did not make a proper answer to it, which gave us cause to suspect
they were not friends. The Sampson and
the Argo were therefore ordered to chase.
The strangers were making a number of
signals, and forming the line of battle first
on one tack, and then on the other repeatedly as though undetermined what to do, our
number and appearance intimidated them
to such a degree, that they could adopt no
settled motions. About ten o'clock we saw
them hoisting a number of signals, and
firing guns; immediately six sail hauled
their wind, and crowded away from us
under a press of sail. Orders were immediately given to prepare for action: the
men of war and Indiamen got into their
respective stations, and all were cleared in

anxious expectation of the event; our
courses were hauled up, and the main-
top-sail aback, so that they came up fast.
As they neared us they hoisted British colours, and made directly for the Lion in
very close order. The headmost ship appeared very large, our imagination painted
her at least a seventy-four, and the other
four fifties, and large frigates. The preceding signal was once more shewn, but
not being answered we made ourselves
certain that they had no friendly intent.
The guns were cast loose and loaded; but
our lower-deck ports were kept close, till
they had got nearly within reach of our
shot, when they were hauled up, the guns
run out, the matches lighted, and every
man at his station. About twelve o'clock,
the headmost ship run alongside of us,
and proved to be the Assistance of fifty
guns; the other four were Indiamen, and
the six smaller ships, the Orpheus, Co-
met, Echo, Latona, Mercury, and Hol-
derness, which stood away to windward,

were taken up to bring sugar from Bengal. The Assistance was to convoy them to St. Helena, or the Cape of Good Hope, and bring the homeward bound ships back: but falling in with us, she here left them to pursue their voyage to India alone (there being no danger to be apprehended from the enemy in those seas), and joined our fleet. By her we learnt that the British fleet, under Lord Howe, had gained a complete victory over the French, and had destroyed and taken several of their first rates, without much loss on our side; and we were happy to find that the seas were scoured in such a manner, that our enemies had not a sufficient number of ships at sea, to offer to intercept this valuable fleet, of which they certainly had pretty good intelligence, though the people in the Assistance told us, that we were not expected to leave St. Helena till the latter end of this month, and that no information had arrived respecting the Lion,

or the Embassador's return from China.
In short, I believe, it was the prevailing
opinion, that we should return to Europe
round Cape Horn, which would have length-
ened our absence considerably. Lord Macartney had formerly expressed his wish
to do so; but the war breaking out in Europe, frustrated his intention. The gratification of his own curiosity gave way to
the pleasure of being serviceable to his
country, in times of such emergency. The
Assistance had a copy of our signals, and
took her station in the centre of the fleet;
we had now one 44, one 50, and two 64
gun ships, so that we thought ourselves
able to cope with a pretty large number of Frenchmen, should they be daring
enough to come amongst us. We parted
from the ships for Bengal at dusk, in latitude 12° 30′ north, and about 20° west
longitude. The Sir Edward Hughes fired
a gun, and hoisted his pendent as Commodore, after the departure of the Assist-

ance; they stood away S E, and we N N W,
a fresh breeze from the N E, and fine clear
weather.

The line of battle ahead, as formed on
the 21st.

Starboard tack on board.

H. M. S. Sampson, 64 guns, 600 men.
Comp. ship Glatton,
Exeter,
Warley,
Osterly,
Lord Walsingham,
General Coote,
Fitzwilliam,
Portugueze Bon Jesus, 26 guns, 130 men.
Spanish   King Charles, 34 guns, 160
men.
H. M. S.   Lion, 64 guns, 400 men.
Comp. ship Royal Charlotte,
Fort William,
Marquis of Lansdown,

Comp. ship Earl of Abergavenny,

Hindostan,

Henry Dundas,

Ceres,

Hawke,

Triton,

Belvidere,

H. M. S. Argo, 44 guns, 350 men.

July 25th, calms and light airs of variable winds. Caught several small fish, a dolphin, and a large porpoise.

On the 26th, the Sampson, about half a cable's length to leeward of us, made a signal that a man had fallen overboard: the ' life buoy' was cut adrift, and two men, who were pretty good swimmers, followed it, and they had the good fortune to save him, there being but little wind, and the sea very smooth.

On the 27th, we were still in the same

tantalizing situation, with respect to wind and weather. For the last fortnight we had not made more than two or three degrees on our proper course. By the most accurate reckoning, we were in 13° north latitude, and about 25° west longitude, St. Jago bearing N N E about fifty leagues. On the evening of the 27th, Francis Vincent, seaman, fell down the main hatchway, and fractured his skull in so dreadful a manner, that he expired in great agonies a few hours afterwards.

On the 28th, a fresh breeze sprung up from the N E, which continued invariable till we were within the Tropics. The 1st of August it blew very fresh, about noon the main-top-sail yard snapt just in the slings, and the sail split in pieces; the top men were all aloft, but happily none were hurt, and another yard was soon rigged. We crossed the Tropic of Cancer on the

5th, in 34° west longitude. The Argo and
the Bon Jesus lost each a man overboard
this day.

On the 6th, the wind veered round to the
south-east; made the signal to steer north
by west. On the same day we saw a few
birds, and a quantity of sea weed floating
round the ship, though at least 200 leagues
from the Canary Islands, which was the
nearest land to us, bearing west by north;
but I understood afterwards it came from
the Gulf of Florida, and is called gulf
weed; we saw it in vast quantities for above
a week. On the 7th, the Lucas south sea
whaler had a boat swamped in chasing a
whale. On the 8th, made the signal for the
fleet to steer north-north-east; and the
same day an officer from each man of war
met on board the Assistance to hold a
survey on her provisons, which they found
to be bad, and much damaged. We be-

gan to be rather in want of a fresh supply ourselves, being on short allowance,
and that of a very indifferent quality.

From the 8th to the 12th of August, we
had calms and light airs of wind. We
employed every day, when the weather
would permit, in exercising the lower deck
guns.

On the 12th, at daybreak, we discovered
a strange sail in the north-east quarter,
standing to the eastward. The Sampson
was ordered to chase; and at 2 P. M. he
shewed the stranger's signal, but being at
so great a distance we could not properly
distinguish it. At 5 P. M. her signal was
hoisted to return into her station.

On the 20th we fell in with a Danish
ship from India, who informed our captain
that she had been overhauled by a French
squadron only three days before, and told

us, that they inquired very particularly after our fleet, how long we had been at sea, and our number; but when he told them we sailed from St. Helena a fortnight before him, and consisted of two line of battle ships and a frigate, they seemed to think it was as well they did not meet with us; they were one ship of 80 guns, three frigates, and a sloop of war.

In the Channel we fell in with the grand fleet, under the command of Earl Howe (waiting for the French); it was in the night, and very dark, and blowing hard. Some of the men of war run foul of several of our Indiamen, considerably damaged them; one was totally dismasted, and obliged to put into Plymouth to repair her damage.

On the 6th of September, 1794, we came to an anchor at the long wished for port, Spithead, after a long, troublesome, tedious, and unhealthy voyage. Both soldiers and sailors had suffered innumerable hardships, and many of each had fallen victims to a cruel disorder (the flux), which had raged on board the Lion with great violence. Since our leaving Batavia (on the 17th of March, 1793), we had buried from the Lion alone near ninety seamen, and seven officers. Out of his Lordship's guard we had lost three artillery men, one infantry, and one of our light dragoons, (Adam Bradshaw) and most of the rest were very weak, and fitter for the hospital than a march, or the fatigues of a campaign; but we were in hopes our native country, and nourishing diet, would soon restore us to perfect health again.

On the 8th we disembarked with joyful hearts I believe, for a pleasing countenance appeared in every man's face, thinking in a few minutes to step upon our native soil once more, and bid adieu to the briny main; and no one regretted their departure from the ship; and we said to each other, we should think but trifling of the hardships of soldiering hereafter, having so severely felt that of sailoring.

THE END.